Make Money Owning Your Car (and enjoy every minute!)

NEW EDITION

John R. Olson

Motorbooks International
Publishers & Wholesalers Inc.
Minneapolis

ISBN: 0-87938-027-6
Library of Congress Catalog Card Number: 75-34302

First published by John R. Olson, 1973. Revised, updated and enlarged by Motorbooks International Publishers & Wholesalers, Inc., 1976.

Printed in the United States of America.

Library of Congress Cataloging in Publication Data
Olson, John R
   Make money owning your car (and enjoy every minute!)
   Includes bibliographical references and index.
   1. Automobile purchasing. I. Title.
TL162.O43 1976 629.22'22 75-34302
ISBN 0-87938-027-6

This edition is dedicated
To those of you
Who find pleasure in investments
You can use rather than just watch and count.

Above — **1953 STUDEBAKER STARLINER** Below — **1970 CHEVROLET CAMARO:** In all products, a few designs defy obsolescence. The two cars on this page were introduced in two separate decades, yet both remain as attractive today, in a third decade, as when they were first conceived.

Preface

Homes go up in value, if reasonably maintained — cars do not! For this reason cars become the most costly purchase in the family budget. This book suggests a way to end the high cost of car ownership and begin treating your automobile as a permanent asset, as you would a home. It shows how your car *can* increase in value. Your local new car dealer is not apt to suggest this book's idea, so read on and consider a new approach in your next car purchase.

In a recent issue of *The Wall Street Journal*,[1] Peter Drucker described six common economic fallacies. One about the automobile reveals that cars drop in value much faster than they wear out. According to his analysis, Americans frequently trade in their new cars after a year or two, ditto for the second owner; as a result, the first owner pays about twice as much per mile as the third owner if total expenses are included. Drucker ranks this unplanned phenomenon as the most effective form of 'income distribution' we have in the United States.

I would suggest three other myths:

The Service-Problem Myth. Most people sell their cars out of fear that big repairs are just ahead. Owners of older cars report just the opposite: that it takes 30,000 miles or so just to get the bugs out of a car, and a long period of happy motoring lies ahead.

The Social-Status Myth. For a long time, automotive ads have been trying to convince people that when you drive home in a new car the whole neighborhood is going to line up along your block 'oohing' and 'aahing.' If that's what you want, you ought to try driving home in a 1953 Studebaker hardtop.

The No-Parts Myth. "Sure it's pretty, but where would I ever get parts for it?" Every old-car owner has heard that question, and every veteran old-car owner knows the answer. There are people all over the country in the business of buying out dealer's stocks of old parts and selling them piecemeal as N.O.S. (new old stock). More on this in the book.

The financial merits of this book's suggestions stand on their own without obliging you to take up another hobby. On the other hand, serious car collectors will find little if anything new in this book; some charts are original, but the philosophy and concepts are elementary — a rationale and invitation for new enthusiasts. It won't surprise me if some of you find driving and preserving automobiles becomes the most economical hobby you pursue. Spreading this information will not diminish its validity — the actual impact it has on the marketplace should be positive. So you're all welcome!

Much has been written lately about the future of the automobile, its pollution and fuel consumption liabilities. Congested streets and highways are also impetus for major reassessments. Gasoline-powered automobiles will be with us for many years, but if they eventually go the way of the horse, their dollar value will be higher than ever, especially for well preserved examples from any manufacturer. Change will be slow. Alternatives have to be incredibly brilliant before people change their habits (even when coaxed by legislation). And if alternative transportation does occur, people will keep their cars for the same reason they still keep horses. Some of them give a great deal of pleasure. Some of them are things of beauty — moving sculpture!

The automobile is a recent invention in man's history. Early examples, be they the first with four-wheel brakes, or the first with computerized anti-skid braking systems, will all be museum-worthy in the next century. I am convinced that the automobile has had the greatest single impact of any invention on Western civilization — the mobile civilization. Historians and museums will be hard-pressed to show anything with broader ramifications for twentieth century lifestyles than our automobiles. Just this year several prominent national museums announced that they are expanding the scope of items displayed to include those more relevant to their patronage.

The New York Museum of Modern Art has had automobiles on exhibit almost continuously for more than two decades.

It has been gratifying to prepare this new edition, as the book's essential premise did not need to be changed. It is more desirable today than ever to stop treating cars as disposable objects. My information indicates increased respect for used cars, and longer-term ownership is already occuring. Auto parts stores nationwide have experienced sensationally increased business in replacement parts, and the pricing of quality used cars is also up. There is expanding evidence that those of you who determine to convert your car(s) into permanent assets will find it possible. Happy driving *and* investing!

John R. Olson
Minneapolis
January, 1976

Table of Contents

1 New Car Costs and Depreciation

A recent *Better Homes and Gardens* magazine had a widely-read article entitled "A Second Car that Pays for Itself." It reported that many post-WW II cars "are modern in every important aspect of safety and performance . . . [and] increasing in value every day you drive. . . ."[2]

Can this be true? In many instances it is; giving you further information on how it happens, and how you can do it too, is the objective of this book. There is a common misconception about this subject which I'd like to address in the beginning. It's one thing to have a car that appreciates, as we all hope will also happen to our homes. It's quite another thing to buy a $1,500 auto and have it "now worth more than $20,000," which was the case of one Mr. Sidney Farnsworth's Bentley, as reported in the September 1973 issue of *Fortune*.[3] This case is an extreme example of the principles described in this book. All the factors mentioned later must be in perfect tune to achieve it . . . and even then this extravagant appreciation may not

take place. These pages will take a more conservative, more frequently achievable tack.

The new car purchaser's plight is 'in-
stitutionalized depreciation.' I will show you
how this loss can be generally reversed, without
loss of vehicle reliability, to the point of recovering maintenance costs and actually making a
few dollars, if that is your objective. That in
itself should please most owners. Going after
big rewards involves the same variables, though
tolerances become stiffer, and 'enjoying every
minute' becomes harder. Thus, by definition,
large investment gains are outside the scope of
this book.

Having defined the limits of our subject,
let's look for a few minutes at the costs most of
us are already encountering with our regular,
newly purchased cars.

New car sales have frequently exceeded
ten million units per year in the United States.
The average price for standard-sized cars is
now more than $4,400. For compact cars, it is
more than $3,500. The average duration of
first ownership is three years. A recent Department of Transportation study states that the
first year's depreciation for standard-sized cars
is $1,046; second year's average, — $647; third
year — $550, totaling $2,243 over the first
three years![4] This means that a standard-sized
three-year-old trade-in is worth $2,157 on the
average (half are worth less). Financing for the
cash difference between a three-year-old car
and a new one ($2,243) at a ten percent interest
rate is $487. Result: $2,243 depreciation plus
$487 interest equals $2,730 before any operat-

ing costs are counted . . . a stiff price even without the interest.

Why do people buy new cars? It's easier to answer that question without the $2,730 cost hanging in front of us, but let's try:

(1) "It's better to buy (own) a new car because the trouble I could have with a used one isn't worth the grief."

(2) "There's nothing like taking the wheel of a new car."

(3) "The low caliber of mechanics in this country precludes keeping a car once it starts to give trouble."

You could add to the list, but surely two key reasons are the joys of driving a new car and escape from mechanical worries.

People who buy a new car every three years for a period of ten years (with no allowance for inflation) will spend $9,091 on depreciation and interest before counting any gas or insurance.

Folks who trade every two years pay an average of $9,777 (depreciation and interest) for their peace of mind during the ten-year period.

The subject gets more painful when the Minnesota Office of Consumer Services reports that sixty-four percent of all new car purchasers in its study had some kind of trouble with their cars during their first year of ownership.[5] Fifty-one percent of these troubles were within the first thirty days, and seventy percent within the first ninety days. More than half of those with trouble said the difficulties were not corrected on the first visit back to the dealer.

One out of every three owners with trouble was without his car for three or more days during repairs. A third of the owners reported having to return to their dealer four or more times, and twenty-one percent of the owners never did get satisfaction!

How is our list of reasons for buying new cars doing by now? A new car is like our dreams. Some are good and some aren't so good. In fact, I hope your dreams are more often satisfactory than the percentage of satisfaction reported for new car owners!

There is a fundamental difficulty obtaining competent service for new or used cars, the quality of new car engineering and assembly notwithstanding. When inferior service strikes us, it costs as much for our time spent as for our money. It should be blatantly clear that the inadequate diagnostic work and incompetent servicemen (or conflicting incentives for mechanics to achieve our objectives) are at the core of a serious national problem which preys on the average motorist. He is willing to spend $1,046-plus in depreciation over the course of his one-year new car warranty to escape car troubles and the unsatisfying service that breakdowns precipitate. The irony is that he doesn't escape. Obviously the warranty is worth something, but not in excess of $1,000 per year! In ten years that would restore and rebuild every detail of most cars twice! The $1,693 (over two years on depreciation alone) gives half of all new car buyers about one new design feature and a shinier package of troubles, together with a skimpier warranty than

CHRYSLER TOWN AND COUNTRY 8: Above, 1946 convertible; below, 1950 Newport hardtop. A whole series of 'woodies' by Chrysler began before WW II. Nash, Mercury and Ford also sold several body types on this theme. All are desirable cars today if the wood is flawlessly maintained or replaced in authentic tone and grain. Painting the wood is strictly out of order! These Chryslers are especially pleasant to drive due to their smooth 323.5-cubic inch straight-eights and Fluid-Drive semi-automatic transmissions. 1946-48 wheelbase: 127.5 inches; 1949-50 wheelbase: 131.5 inches.

the vehicle being traded in had. Remember that a few years ago factory warranties lasted five years.

Later in this book is a section which may help you with service, undoubtedly the most critical problem facing new as well as used-car owners today. Mechanics receive much more of our money annually than most nations' physicians and hospitals combined. Why isn't the fraternity of mechanics even one-fourth as professional? It is my feeling that the conflict of interest in pay sources for repairmen is the largest single problem. Many mechanics don't get to know car owners, since they receive work through their bosses, the service managers. Many mechanics receive commissions on parts replaced, in addition to their base pay. At a minimum, parts commissions should be outlawed!

To summarize, the *new* car buyer can depend on three big bills before he even counts his operating expenses:

    (1) Substantial depreciation.

    (2) Interest on time purchase costs.

    (3) Unwarrantied but required service, and time lost on repeat visits for adjustments.

2 Long Term Car Values

The rate of depreciation for standard sedans and compact-sized cars is a curiosity in itself. The loss (except in cases of hard usage) is not proportionate to the remaining life potential of a competently maintained vehicle.

These charts are composites of many brands, with differing beginning years, so individual models may be slightly different . . . but the pattern is there, and it's hard to break out of the pattern, regardless of what car you own. Dealers won't help — they put you into it.

AVERAGE DEPRECIATION RATES OVER TEN YEARS

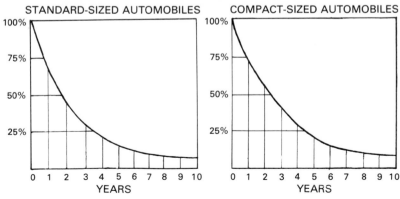

STANDARD-SIZED AUTOMOBILES   COMPACT-SIZED AUTOMOBILES

As recently as 1955, Jack Spiegel of Philadelphia advertised his 1935 V-16 Cadillac with six wire wheels for $300 in *Road & Track* magazine. A 1930 Rollston-bodied Duesenberg in excellent condition was offered in the same issue for $2,500 by a gentleman near Miami. Fifteen years later neither car could be touched

1940 DUESENBERG: This unusual SJ town car currently in the W. Pettit Collection dramatizes Duesenberg's size and strength. Note the three hinges on each door, atypical front fenders and the special radiator. Duesenberg used a straight-eight engine of 420 cubic inches with double overhead valves and four valves per cylinder. When a supercharger was applied to this engine the standard 320 hp rose to 400 hp. Maximum speed was 125-plus mph; weight was 6,500 lb. Wheelbase: 153.5 inches.

for ten times those figures! Where is the pattern? How can we all make better car ownership decisions with this information?

The National Market Report's *Red Book* doesn't help. These used-car value guides tend to stop listing cars after the sixth year, by which time they have methodically reported each car's demise to near zero value. But something is missing from these bibles of the used car industry. The last year that the *Red Book* listed the following cars, they gave the accompanying average retail prices for examples in good condition with full accessories; I've added another ten percent for 'mint' condition.

Year and Model	Last Year and Price Recorded		Average 1975 Value	% Annual Increase In Value, Compounded
53 Buick Skylark	1960	$ 315	$3,200	16.71% per year
53 Chevrolet Corvette	1966	1,150	6,800	21.83% per year
53 Packard Caribbean	1960	600	3,800	13.09% per year
54 Lincoln Capri	1961	360	2,300	14.16% per year
55 Chrysler 300	1963	350	4,000	22.50% per year
55 Ford Thunderbird	1963	1,125	5,600	14.30% per year
57 Chevrolet Nomad	1964	775	2,750	12.20% per year
59 Ford Retractable Hdtp.	1967	575	2,100	15.47% per year
63 Avanti-Studebaker	1966	2,040	4,400	10.08% per year
63 Lincoln Continental Conv.	1970	1,000	3,250	26.58% per year

Try to buy any of these cars today. Oh, they're available, but the center column shows the price that will be necessary to acquire one in good condition today. These prices are climbing steeply each year.

DEPRECIATION/REAPPRECIATION CHART

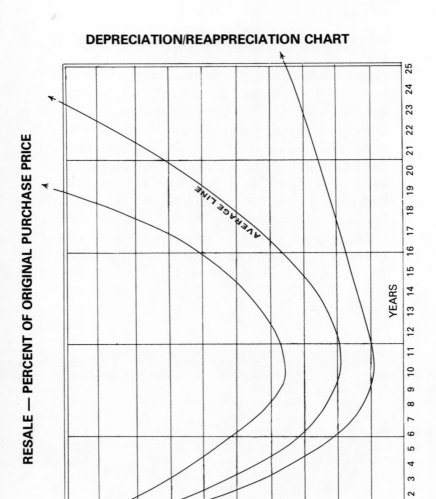

The above chart is startling. It averages the selling prices of good-condition cars in our first list, plus thirteen other collectible cars,[6] as reported in the pages of *Hemmings Motor News, Cars & Parts, Kruse Auction Record Book* and sales I've personally witnessed during the past few years. While this is a selected list of cars, with a mixture of seventy-five percent selling prices and twenty-five percent asking prices, I am confident it is a realistic reflection of what is happening to vehicle values. Few cars will recover their original selling price precisely on the twenty-fifth year, and favored models go up faster; but the general pattern is easily confirmable by anyone who wants to do additional research.

Obviously, it is difficult to report specific prices here, since they are changing very quickly. I do so only to explain the phenomenon. What does this do to the *Red Book* depreciation charts? It does a lot to them that new car dealers never support. It turns their charts

1937 SUPERCHARGED CORD 812 PHAETON: The 810-812 Cord models were designed by Gordon M. Buehrig, who also did the Tucker. All Cords featured front-wheel drive and the 810-812 models were powered by a Lycoming L-head V-8 with 288.6 cid; producing 130 hp in the blown versions. Most 810-812's had a 125-inch wheelbase and they weighed about 4,000 pounds. Many replicas of these latter models have been manufactured, but the unmodified original is clearly the most desirable.

upside down during the second ten to twelve years!

Scarcity strongly increases these values for any make of car. This is examined closely at the beginning of Chapter 5. Let me say here to not let scarcity frighten you. The low survival rate of any mass-produced car gives rise to a trail of parts sources in every state; a whole subculture of service, parts and enthusiasts emerge for nearly every car ever built. This becomes important, as part of a 'new' conventional wisdom we should have sufficiently confirmed by the time you finish this book. That is the wisdom (indeed, advantage) of maintaining a five-year old car, or a ten-year

CHRYSLER 300: This 1955 model is the first of seven years of 300's. A total of 1,704 models were built in 1955, all hardtops available only in white, red or black. Applying the chart in Chapter 4 to these cars, less than two dozen remain on the highway today. A total of 1,356 convertibles and 9,140 hardtops were built. All had full leather; many had air conditioning. A few hundred (1958 only) were equipped with Bendix fuel injection. Top speed was 130-140 mph. Wheelbase: 126 inches.

old car, in eighty-five to ninety percent of its original condition and performance capability!

Some will be restless with this kind of reasoning. Won't it cost a fortune in time and money to keep a used car in high operating condition for over ten years, and who would want its obsolete features then, anyway?

A fortune to keep it running . . . recall for a minute the price ten million Americans spend to keep *new* cars rolling that first two years, and cumulatively for ten years! Those dollars don't even touch maintenance expenses. On a budget of $2,400 every two years, visualize how smart your 'older' automobile would look and perform! In fact, there is *no* earthly reason why you need spend even $1,000 per year (at 1974's cost of living) on maintenance. Eight to ten percent of a new car's purchase price, per year, is a generous figure to allow for maintaining an older car. Your old car can hold and increase its value, giving distinctive, contemporary transporta-

1955-56 IMPERIAL: Ahhh . . . a post-WW II dual-cowl phaeton! Chrysler built several of these cars in 1953, 1955 and 1956; some are presently owned by large cities for parade use. Los Angeles still uses theirs frequently.

tion to boot. Except for printed circuits and the newest safety features (some of which should be added), no significant technological or convenience features have been added to cars that were not available in the fifties.

As for obsolescence, this book's pages include pictures of specific cars, listing the features they offer . . . far from obsolete.

My mother has been driving an interesting car the past few summers. She is in her seventies, so a prerequisite was power steering, power brakes and automatic transmission. She wanted a safe, reliable car, one that was quiet, handled well and offered good visibility. That should be easy. Many cars meet these requirements, from Chevrolet to Mercedes-Benz.

Let me list some of the features of the car she has been using:

> Factory air-conditioning
> Substantial insulation for quietness
> High-torque, low rpm V-8 engine
> Four-way power seats
> Tinted glass all around
> Electric windows
> Dual heating system
> Long range radio
> Power steering
> Power brakes
> Automatic transmission
> Leather upholstery
> Safety features included:
> Backup lights, non-glare rear mirror, outside mirror, windshield washers, safety belts, safety tires

Seems like a normal list of features for any of a dozen current models; however, the one she has driven is a 1954 Lincoln Capri sedan. It had 28,000 miles when I bought it, and at this writing, counting original cost and cumulative maintenance work, I have $2,500 invested in it. The only item I've added to the car is the safety belts. I regard it as every bit as reliable for my mother's use as a brand new car — probably more reliable based on the study described earlier.

Some of you will feel $2,500 is way too much to spend for any 1954 automobile. I can understand your reaction, as the upswing of the value curve is hard to absorb as fact until you actually see it happen several times. There is little doubt in my mind that, kept in peak condition, this Lincoln will regain its original selling price value of $5,200 (it has air-conditioning) in a few more years. And even if it does not, where else can I buy a full luxury automobile with all accessories, capable of age-less prestige in town and high-speed touring on the expressway, for $2,500?

How high is up? My curves on the Depreciation/Reappreciation Chart in this chapter rise toward the sky. There is a demarcation point at which cars, like other objects of art and history, rise above their intrinsic value in mortar, paint and metal; this point confirms in dollars what people's hearts express in admiration.

But why cars? Leave our hobby to obscurity, and focus on other things? Impossible. The automobile is probably the greatest single symbol of our modern, technologically-obsessed civilization.

Thousands of examples from thirty-plus centuries of fine art make the legacy of a few decades of collectible cars seem small by comparison. However, Jim Southard of Atlanta, Georgia, predicted in 1973 that we will see cars worth $1 million in years to come. Surprisingly, that's more conservative than it sounds. In 1975 I wrote an article in *Old Cars* newspaper suggesting that none of the present owners of the six Bugatti Royales would put their cars on the market for $1 million.[7] None

1970 MANIC GT: While the average Canadian car buff already preserves a Meteor or Bricklin, this Quebec product should attract more collectors in years to come: It was powered by a ninety-eight cubic inch (1600 cc) power plant that put out 170 hp at 7800 rpm! Linked with a five-speed transmission, four-wheel disc brakes, torsion bar suspension and an eighty-one-inch wheelbase — the nickname could become 'greased lightning.' The body was glass over a welded multi-tubular chassis.

of the owners responded, in effect declining an implicit offer.

Does it stop with the Bugatti? The late Lance Reventlow attempted to buy one of the eight authentic Mercedes-Benz 300SLR straight-eight racing cars before he built his highly successful Scarabs. Mercedes-Benz wouldn't even let him see the blueprints. Finally, Ford allowed Reventlow's engineers — together with Ford engineers, who were equally interested — to disassemble, measure, photograph, and reassemble key parts of the 300SLR owned by Ford's Greenfield Museum. Care to speculate what it would take to buy one of these cars? Current high auction prices do not approach the real value of dozens of cars that may not change owners for fifty years. The open secret is, great cars are already treasured as fine art . . . three-dimensional art of the finest caliber.

3 Specific Cars That Will Reappreciate

Many excellent, low-mileage cars are crying to be discovered as they pass down through the $2,000 level toward $1,000 and below. While these cars will take longer to reappreciate than the Lincoln described in the last chapter, they have other benefits which make their further depreciation ludicrous. I've included a good share of these cars among the photos in this book, as I suspect they are the cars in which a majority of the readers of this book will have an interest . . . and their reappreciation potential is very good.

All of these cars have promising long-term futures, and should deliver above-average driving pleasure, if they are kept on a responsible maintenance schedule. They are above-average motorcars and they deserve peak maintenance and a destiny of love. They will appreciate in value in return. There are many others too, that space does not allow me to include. Note the number of compact and semi-compact-sized cars from the 1960's in this group.

The significant automotive developments of the sixties, as in any decade, were few. I believe that history will be kind to the better compact cars that emerged in the sixties, for example, the GM efforts: Buick's Special and Skylark introduced America's first V-6 and a 350-pound aluminum V-8; Oldsmobile's F-85 and Chevrolet's rear engine Corvair offered turbocharged carburetion; and Pontiac's original LeMans had a transaxle (rear transmission with front engine) and flexible drive shaft. I understand the drive shaft was a disaster, but it's a shame we don't have the transaxle today.

1961 OLDSMOBILE F-85: This was the first Oldsmobile compact car available in two-door, four-door and station wagon (with a roof-hinged tailgate) models (1961). Nineteen sixty-two added a very desirable convertible. Buick, as usual, produced companion-sized cars, equally sensible and significant to the collector. The series was powered by an all-aluminum, water-cooled, 215-cubic inch V-8 engine. Weighing only 350 pounds, it delivered 155 horsepower. By 1963 it had climbed to 200 hp in Buick's Skylark. The tooling for this engine was sold in 1966 to Rover of England and is still used in the 3.5-liter V-8 offered by Rover and the Morgan Plus-8. It is alleged that GM tried unsuccessfully to buy the tooling back in 1973.

1965 OLDSMOBILE 442: Pontiac, Oldsmobile and Buick all offered compact muscle cars beginning in 1965. Pontiac's LeMans (GTO) got the most publicity, though some reports attributed better suspension characteristics to the Oldsmobile. Four-four-two (4-4-2) originally stood for four-barrel carburetor, four-speed shift and dual exhausts. The car was soon offered with automatic drive, too. With the recent speed and pollution restrictions, manufacturers may not build power plants of this size much longer: V-8, 400 cubic inches, 435 ft-lb of torque and 335 hp. Wheelbase: 112 inches. Did you ever see a 1964-65 Olds F-85 rust out at the wheel wells? Your author hasn't. GM knows how to end rust, but this special inner fender design was quietly dropped after a couple of years. Too good to keep?

1966 OLDSMOBILE TORONADO: One of the most functionally beautiful large automobiles in the world. Its lines are solidly legitimate in origin — the wheel wells, roof line, naturally-flowing window line and bumpers all confirm their existence with a handsome sense of purpose. These features are timeless; an equally beautiful but nonfunctional fin or elaborately curved slab or chrome is not. Yet the changes that have occurred on the Toronado since 1966 have 'watered down' its distinctiveness in each successive year. The current models have entirely lost their decisive body shape. Why the changes? "Change is what sells," remarks a dealer. Collectors generally do not carry these confused values into their collections. Wheelbase: 119 inches.

Sales failed to offset the mounting costs of producing these creations; but that is not to GM's discredit as much as to the public's for not buying more of these constructive new product designs. GM persevered, introducing the overhead-cam Pontiac six, and the front-wheel drive Oldsmobile and Cadillac. All of these cars are prime candidates for collectors. The early Mustangs, though mechanically very conventional, have a good future. The Rambler American, Valiant and Dart convertibles are already rare.

As with anything else, there are exceptions, but legitimate improvements in engineering (as distinguished from cost reduction changes) take no reliable pattern of appearance. New car announcements only occa-

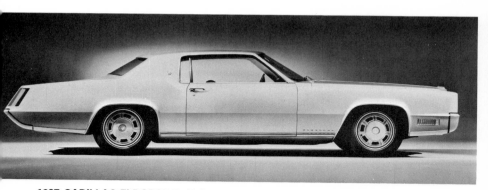

1967 CADILLAC ELDORADO: Following Oldsmobile's Toronado by one year, this 120-inch wheelbase beauty confirmed GM's commitment to front-wheel drive vehicles. Mammoth engine size challenged the belief that universal joints required for front-wheel power were only suited to small engines. At 429 cubic inches (seven liters), this Eldorado delivered 340 hp and 480 ft-lb of torque at a mere 3000 rpm. It should be noted that enthusiasts distinguish among Cadillacs worth saving. While ready to restore the 1957-60 Eldorado Brougham and convertibles in general, collectors tend to pay markedly lower prices for sedans unless they are air conditioned. During the past twenty-four months, prices of all well-preserved Cadillacs have been climbing faster than market averages.

sionally mean improvements for consumers. Even when improvements do occur, collectors tend to prefer the first year of a series. There's no question that Zora Arkus-Duntov's mechanical improvements enhanced the second series (1956 and later) Chevrolet Corvettes . . . though the highest prices are commanded by the original 1953-55 body design.

Most people think of luxury cars when collector cars are envisoned, though among the post-war 'greats,' original cost has had much less correlation with luxury status than is the case for pre-WW II cars recognized by the

1965 FORD MUSTANG: Similar to Chevrolet, public demand for old Ford convertibles is intense. Since the 1965 model was the first of the highly successful Mustangs, how can it fail to be a key representative of Ford history? As this book is published, a 1965 model in excellent condition can be purchased for $1,500 and less, nationwide. In this writer's opinion, the Mustang is a perfect example of a car that will triple, maybe quadruple, in value in a few years. Don't grab the first one to limp over the hill. Insist on no rust, good chrome, interior and engine. Weak examples sell for $350 and less; but you won't get to third base trying to restore one for less than $1,500, so save your money for a good Mustang. The V-8 is preferable to the six-cylinder, but authenticity (proper color and upholstery) should be the decisive factor in making your choice.

1953 CHEVROLET CORVETTE: Recognized by many Corvette enthusiasts to be a fresh, flowing, thoroughly modern design with one of the few attractive wraparound windshields (accomplished to some extent by omitting roll-up side windows, which were added in 1956). The Corvette was first offered with only six-cylinder power and automatic drive; they had 150 hp via triple carburetion. In 1955, a V-8 engine was added to the same body. The body was rust-proof, dent-proof, glass-reinforced plastic. These early Corvettes, despite their modest engines, command remarkable resale values today — well above the original dealer price of $3,560. The 1956-57 edition had Zora Arkus-Duntov's camshaft, four-speed transmission, fuel injection and a new suspension, wholly changing the car's personality. In 1957, Corvette broke the Mercedes-Benz 300SL's Bonneville record, and achieved 150.583 mph in Daytona's Flying Mile Speed Records. Wheelbase: 102 inches. Production: 300 in 1953; 3,640 in 1954; 9,231 in 1955; 8,103 in 1956; 6,264 in 1957. The 1963-64 fastback Sting Ray model is also a Corvette to watch.

1963 CORVETTE STING RAY SPORTS COUPE: Chevrolet's 1963 'split-window' Corvette coupe has phenomenal appeal among Corvette buffs. In the long run, all Corvettes preserved in original condition will have strong appeal to collectors. Since one third of all cars sold are Chevrolets, the nostalgia for older 'top-of-the-line' models is always strong. Wheelbase of all 1963-67 models was ninety-eight inches.

Classic Car Club of America. Volkswagen has shown that body integrity and good paint work are not confined to costly cars. Mercedes-Benz has shown that great expressway performance does not require huge weight and engine size.

The 1962-67 Buick Skylark series may be one of the 'sleepers' of the decade . . . and accordingly is an example of a good buy. Average in original price ($4,000 in equipped form), these well-assembled, road-worthy motorcars show as much space efficiency and have as many luxury appointments as any car $2,500 above their original price. The body design wears well: It is soft-spoken, balanced and

1966 FORD THUNDERBIRD: The four-passenger T-Birds have a spottier acceptance among collectors than the two-seat models, though two other forces will probably overcome this resistance: Ford's strong following among old car buffs, and the likelihood that convertibles of every make will be at a premium soon. The recent (1968-72) Thunderbird four-door sedans (especially those with sun roofs and factory air-conditioning) are worth consideration, too. Their size defies the assumption that T-Birds must be small; yet these four-door carriages were the smallest luxury sedans offered in the U.S. Optional on the 1966 model was a 428-cid V-8 producing 345 hp — standard was a 315-hp, 390-cid V-8.

thoroughly contemporary. I had occasion to drive one with factory air-conditioning on a 2,000 mile trip a few years ago, and came back feeling it had behaved like a $10,000 luxury car. It was quiet, fast, and had a silky-smooth transmission. Some critics say Buicks ride too softly. Nothing prevents the installation of some good stiff shock absorbers . . . and they'll accomplish more on a car of the Skylark's size than a full-sized Detroiter.

To keep the rose-colored glasses off, these Buicks have a 'genetic' weakness with which most GM cars of the mid-sixties were plagued: The primer coating of body paint is

1957 FORD THUNDERBIRD: Of the 53,166 T-Birds built from 1954 through 1957, those in authentic condition have now reappreciated beyond their original selling price. For 1954, a 160-horsepower engine with 256-cubic inch displacement, four-barrel carburetor and dual exhaust were featured. Hardtops and soft tops were available. Wheelbase: 102 inches. The introduction of Ford's T-Bird and Chevrolet's Corvette were milestones for the large American manufacturers. These early cars shared many components from standard models, though in subsequent years the reverse has been true, with engine options and new body lines appearing first on sportier models. The '57 model, shown, was the last of the two-seaters.

inferior, causing surface chips and surface rust at the slightest bruise.

This brings up repainting, which as a rule should be avoided entirely. Heroic effort should be made to preserve all original paint surfaces. Cars with original paint, all else being equal, will bring a higher price than slightly shinier, repainted vehicles. The reason is that repaint jobs generally are inferior in both preparation steps (removal of trim, etc.) and authenticity of finish. Of course, there are exceptions to this rule, but proper repainting is not common. More on body maintenance later.

Most cars from the fifties on were offered with automatic transmissions. Power brakes and power steering became prevalent from 1952 to 1954, and air-conditioning was

1951 CHRYSLER SARATOGA TOWN AND COUNTRY, HEMI V-8: After Willys' all-steel Jeep wagon came Plymouth's 1949 suburban and Chrysler's 1951 Town and Country wagons. A now extremely rare New Yorker Town and Country wagon was also offered. The luxurious sedan-like interiors and Briggs-built bodies were a new treat to the emerging world of station wagon owners. Wheelbase: 131.5 inches; 180 hp.

also available on many medium- and higher-priced cars from 1954 onward. Naturally, top-of-the-line models with a full complement of accessories will hold an edge in value, but any well-kept, rust-free car in original or authentically duplicated condition is of acknowledged value. Recently I attended a concours (beauty contest for cars) which included a 'people's choice' trophy for the best post-WW II car. A 1954 Hudson Wasp (not Hudson's top model) won. It was the best-maintained post-WW II car present and everyone knew it. A prestige car of double the Wasp's original price took second place.

1953 OLDSMOBILE 98 FIESTA CONVERTIBLE: In 1953 nearly all American car makers had show car fever, and began offering limited production models in addition to their one-of-a-kind, car-show originals. Richard Teague, American Motors sytling vp, recalls that designers referred to many of these as 'Ho-hum Specials' because they were not creations from the ground up, but merely modified standard models. Teague would include his own 1953-54 Packard Caribbean in the ho-hum category, along with Cadillac's 1953 Eldorado, the 1953 Buick Skylark and Oldsmobile's Fiesta convertible. The Fiesta is the rarest of these cars today. Only six have been located nationwide by the Oldsmobile Club of America membership, and two of these are parts cars. This model had an ohv V-8 of 165 hp; it was the first year of the twelve-volt electrical system. Wheelbase: 124 inches.

4 So You're Not Seeking Another Hobby

Here come the numbers! Budgeteers: Enter here. Buying a new car gains you a warranty, but it also pledges you to a schedule of maintenance, at your expense, to keep the warranty alive. The longest warranty you may recall was five years or 50,000 miles on all drive train parts, offered during the mid-sixties. Detroit figured out that this encouraged extended ownership, which of course didn't help new car sales. Now most warranties are back to twelve months or 12,000 miles on American and imported makes. American Motors does offer a second year's warranty for $90 or $100, though after that you're on your own. That's not as bad as it sounds. A well-conceived maintenance plan will provide you with reliable transporation at controlled, reasonable annual costs for many years. What it takes is the conviction that your dollars are well-placed. To help affirm this in your mind, I've put together the following chart of costs that you will encounter with a new car for five years, versus five years with one of the cars recommended in this book.

The example could be most any car, as I've not made dramatic reappreciation a necessary ingredient. Also, we will assume that there is no trade-in, as it would lower the purchase price of either the new or 'collectible' car by a similar amount. The chart assumes that all maintenance and repairs will be done by a professional mechanic. Gas and insurance will be assumed identical, and therefore self-canceling, costs.

1966 Oldsmobile Toronado		1976 Oldsmobile Toronado	
This car is an original, low (31,000) mileage rust-free example, with all available accessories including air. You located the car through an ad in *Old Cars* newspaper in another state, and spent $200 plus a weekend of your time inspecting and bringing it home: Total cost including the $200 and licensing: $2,400.		This is a comparably equipped model, air, etc., on which you manage to negotiate a moderate discount because it is a showroom model and not the color you really wanted: $7,500.	
First Year: 10,000 miles		**First Year: 10,000 miles**	
Immediate expenses:		Immediate expenses:	
Replace transmission		None	
oil and adjust.	$25		
Two shock absorbers			
(Sears)	$30		
Partial muffler replace-			
ment	$102		
Two good tires	$80		
Subsequent expenses:		Subsequent expenses:	
Tune up	$80	Waxing	$40
Waxing (and touchup)	$40	12 mo. Lub. Schedule	$20
12 mo. Lub. schedule	$20	Tune up	$80
Adjust air cond. & add		Any other service required	
freon	$23	covered by warranty	
Align front suspension	$20		
Total:	$420	Total:	$140

Second Year: 10,000 miles

Replace brake linings and master brake cylinder	$125
Steam clean and re-undercoat	$110
New heater/air cond. motor, add freon	$65
Two good tires	$85
Wax (and touchup)	$45
12 mo. Lub. Schedule	$20
Minor engine tune up	$35
Total:	**$485**

Second Year: 10,000 miles

12 mo. Lub. schedule	$20
Wax	$45
Tune up	$35
Adjust air cond. & add freon	$25
Incidental repairs:	$28
Total	$153

Third Year: 10,000 miles

Grind valves on engine, adjust and tune	$185
Replace transmission	$200
Wax (and touchup)	$45
Adjust air cond. & add freon	$25
Two more shock absorbers	$30
12 month Lubrication	$20
Total:	**$505**

Third Year: 10,000 miles

Major tune up	$100
Repack wheel bearings	$25
Two good tires	$85
Partial muffler system	$80
Replace Alternator	$30
Wax (and touchup)	$45
12 month Lubrication	$20
Total:	**$395**

Fourth Year: 10,000 miles

Replace Alternator	$30
Replace Battery	$35
Replace water pump	$35
Flush radiator, repair system	$100
Repack wheel bearings	$25
12 mo. Lub. Schedule	$20
Major Tune up	$95
Wax	$45
Total:	**$385**

Fourth Year: 10,000 miles

Two good tires	$90
Replace Transmission Fluid & Adjust	$35
Tune up	$45
Wax (and touchup)	$45
Replace Battery	$35
Replace Starter and Solenoid	$56
Repair radio	$35
Adjust air cond. & add freon	$29
12 mo. Lub. Schedule	$20
Total:	**$390**

Fifth Year: 10,000 miles		Fifth Year: 10,000 miles	
Replace Starter & Solenoid	$56	Replace Alternator	$35
Install new universal		Replace brake linings	$85
joints at front wheels,		Major tune up	$90
pack, align front		Repair electric door locks	$34
suspension	$200	Front end alignment	$20
Wax	$50	12 mo. Lub. Schedule	$20
Tune up	$55	Wax	$50
12 mo. Lub. Schedule	$20		
Total:	$381	Total:	$334

Total Five Year		**Total Five Year**	
Maintenance	**$2,276**	**Maintenance**	**$1,412**

At this point the car is sold, also through the cost of three ads in *Old Cars* newspaper; for $2,500. This price might well have been higher, but the 81,000 miles and seller's desire to move the car promptly, led to this price.

At this point the car is sold, through a comparable medium, local advertising, repurchase of another new car, or *Old Cars* newspaper. Based on 50,000 miles and five years of age, $2,500 seems a liberal return.

Result:	Initial Cost	$2,400	Result:	Initial Cost	$7,500
	Maintenance Cost	+2,276		Maintenance Cost	+1,412
		$4,676			$8,912
	Sale Price	−2,500		Sale Price	−2,500
		$2,176			$6,412

$6,412
$2,176

Dollars Gained: $4,236

When a mechanic announces that a transmission needs replacement, or another large repair is necessary, it is rarely budgeted in our normal personal expenses, so we feel pinched by it. And there is no doubt that annual maintenance costs increase with age. In this example, the new car's first-year costs were only $140, growing to $153, $395, $390 and $334 over five years, for an average of $282. The 1966 Toronado averaged $455 per year. Of course, the real message is in the depreciation cost occurring simultaneously on the newly purchased vehicle: $4,236 of dead loss. That amount would cover substantial additional repairs on the 1966 Toronado, or the car could be *given away* at the end of the five years, and you would still be $2,736 ahead!

Lining up the numbers this way makes the larger annual maintenance a path to gaining thousands of dollars rather than losing

1963 BUICK RIVIERA: A departure from standard Buicks, the Riviera was a bold, if heavy, design that has stood up quite well. This first year featured several expensive interior appointments; e.g., full leather and an attractive dash layout that were, unfortunately, economized in 1964. Owners report that the 1964 transmission delivered longer service, so it was a trade-off. Base a purchase on the condition of the individual car rather than on any of these other features. By 1966, significant changes watered down its value to collectors. It was only available as a two-door, with a 117-inch wheelbase; 401-cubic inch V-8, 325-horsepower engine at 4400 rpm. Original price with factory air and power steering: $4,861.

thousands of dollars with no loss of prestige from the experience. A well-maintained older car turns people's heads faster than the new models these days.

The Oldsmobile Toronado in our example is passing through its tenth year on the Reappreciation Chart, so its greatest appreciation potential is yet to come. A car of the Oldsmobile Toronado's age (or newer) is a good investment for those of you who feel more comfortable not going too 'old' on your first venture. These newer cars will give you a greater variety of accessories, particularly *factory* air-conditioning, which is highly desirable whenever you can obtain it. Even if you never use air-conditioning, it will add dramatically

1971-73 BUICK RIVIERA GS: Approximately once every ten years a magnificent Buick is built. The Riviera had provocative front and rear styling. Buick offered exceptional expressway handling and interior quietness. Riviera was given a partial vinyl top, though as a well-proportioned car it didn't need such 'tack-ons.' Shown is a 1973 model: 250 hp V-8 standard with an optional 260 hp — both displaced 455 cid — wheelbase was 122 inches.

(15-25%) to future value. And if you look in this age range, you are more apt to find a well-preserved example somewhere near where you live.

Parts will be available for more routine services for these cars, giving you time to develop contacts with the specialized folks who make a vocation (usually an avocation) of providing parts for your car as it gets older. If you buy from the type of dealer that specializes in collectible cars, age is less of a problem.

I can report from my regular use of cars that are more than ten years old that service is not much different from that of newer cars. Parts sources will change, and you will become an expert on a few of the car's unique features. However, the key is not in doing anything very special . . . just doing everything that's normal; i.e., responsible maintenance.

The longer you have owned a car, the more time you have had to discover its weaknesses; you'll know which components are relatively new and which components you have had installed that carry lifetime guarantees. In all likelihood, you won't hesitate to drive on the expressway to a distant city, because you know the vehicle like your hand.

During the second ten-year period the reappreciation phenomenon gains momentum. The car becomes a prize! Run-of-the-mill examples of your car will literally drop out of sight to become parts cars or food for crushers. Resale value will rise faster than ever if the car is honestly maintained. You will note that the difference between the low and high selling price for any model is almost the same as the restoration cost. Without maintenance, the value slips just like a house that has gone to the dogs. However, it is gratifying to see (and report here) that well-maintained cars will appreciate to a point exceeding the cost of your cumulative maintenance.

Home improvements are often considered good investments. *MONEY* magazine, in a 1973 issue, lists the kinds of house improvements that actually increase the value[8] of the house, as a percent of the improvement's cost.

	Cost:	Value added when home sold:
Attractive recreation room	$1200-2400	$500-1000
Central air-conditioning	$1000-4000	$1000-2000
Upstairs bathroom modernized	$1000-3000	$500-1000
Fully remodeled kitchen	$4000-7000	$1000-2000

Makes you think twice about home improvement expenses! I believe automobile improvement/restoration will easily match or exceed this home appreciation performance before the fifteenth year, and exceed it after the fifteenth year. If we keep our hypothetical 1966 Toronado (which is a very timeless design) beyond the fifteenth year, and drive it 5,000 to 7,000 miles per year, the maintenance costs will likely be less than its rate of reappreciation. Different items will need work, but

$450-$500 (or roughly 8-10% of its original purchase price annually) will keep the car rolling and shining virtually for decades.

These pages come from questioning many car enthusiasts and from my personal experiences driving cars (1) over 100,000 miles, (2) beyond their twentieth year, (3) with more than ten consecutive years' ownership and (4) my eventual selling prices. Contary to 'conventional wisdom,' old cars can deliver fully reliable and economical transportation. Collectors make it happen. You can too. To whatever extent the prices of the cars you seek rise, your selling price will also rise. Greater demand will also improve competition and service and parts sources. Prices are so unrealistically low during most cars' fifth through fifteenth years, that if massive public enlightenment occurred (unlikely), *good* five- to fifteen-year-old cars would still be bargains, even with a fifty percent increase in resale values.

Add a dash (or lump, as the case may be) of annual inflation to all that has been said; and consider that many 'collector' cars will be bought as second or third cars and never see 7,000 miles per year . . . and two more reasons for achieving our objective are found.

To summarize:

(1) Technology improves much more slowly than it changes! (Mr. Richard H. McLean of Newington, Vermont, reports discovering that his early fifties' Hudson Hornet's exhaust is below recent federal pollution limits!)

(2)   The cost of a thorough maintenance schedule for a five- to ten-year-old car is negligible in comparison with a new car's first five years' depreciation; and it is no more inconveniencing than trying to keep the majority of new cars out of the service department.

(3)   Reappreciation does occur.

(4)   You might just meet some other wonderful, independent-thinking people, and have a great deal of fun doing it.

1948 HUDSON COMMODORE CONVERTIBLE: Designed by Robert Andrews, who also created the Avanti, the 'step-down' Hudson was perhaps the most over-constructed car since WW II. Strongly independent in every way, the Hudson Motor Company produced many provocative choices for consumers. As evidenced by the mild acceptance even GM gets for some of its innovations, the public does not seek a great deal of creativity in its motorcars — just slow and/or superficial change (with much fanfare). These 'step-down' Hudsons were built from 1948 through 1954, when the firm slipped hopelessly into red ink. The Hudson-Essex Terraplane Club today has a fervent membership of more than 2,000 nationwide.

5 The Element of Scarcity

The Highway Beautification Act initiated during President Johnson's administration has been followed by aggressive state legislation to clean up our countryside of unsightly billboards and auto junk yards. Most car enthusiasts favor these efforts, though as with everything else, there are instances of overzealous administrators hauling away properly-running, licensed vehicles. Some states are now refining their statutes in recognition of the valid interests of historic car enthusiasts. If you live in a state that has not resolved this matter, your influence with your own elected state officials will ultimately make the difference. Be *sure* they hear from you.

Surprising though it may be, parts sources for even the *rarest* cars are very slow to dry up. Cars in good condition disappear much faster than do parts for them. It is true that after approximately the seventh year, new car dealers generally disown serious responsibility for their own makes. Federal laws protect consumers for only seven years on factory parts. Too many owners tolerate this treatment, just as they submit to low trade-in values; dealers sympathetically point towards a new cycle of depreciation as the only course . . . in other words, a new car. Exit the old car to the junk yard and the crushers.

Registration statistics in any state reveal how many of the new cars sold there get re-registered in subsequent years. G. Marshall Naul, co-founder of the Society of Automotive Historians, reported his research on this subject in *Special-Interest Autos*, April-May, 1972.[9] Essentially, a car's original production volume, be it 50,000 or 500,000, will drop from a 90% survival rate in the third year to 10% survival

1955 CHEVROLET NOMAD: Our museum of station wagons would be incomplete without one of the 1955-57 two-door versions shown here. It brought beauty to a body style that had not previously attracted as much attention as the sedan, hardtop, convertible and sports car designs. Detroit finally discovered, in 1955, that station wagons need not be lumber wagons. Sales of wagons have subsequently grown to the point where only two makes — Cadillac and Lincoln — can afford to ignore the station wagon market. The Nomad had 170 horsepower; more powerful options were available, including fuel injection in 1957. Many of the cars shown in this book were commonly equipped with automatic drive, power steering and power brakes; a few Nomads also had factory air-conditioning and electric windows. Wheelbase: 115 inches.

in the twelfth year, and 1% by the sixteenth year. The following chart is a composite of most of the American automobiles initially registered between 1946 and 1968. The grey area is the probable range within which most models fall. Cars disappearing the fastest are Nash, Hudson, and Plymouth, while those lasting the longest are Cadillac and Chevrolet. Obviously there are some exceptions to this. A few cars are recognized as worth saving as soon as they are built. The 1955 Chevrolet Nomad, now

CAR REGISTRATIONS PERCENT OF ORIGINAL PRODUCTION

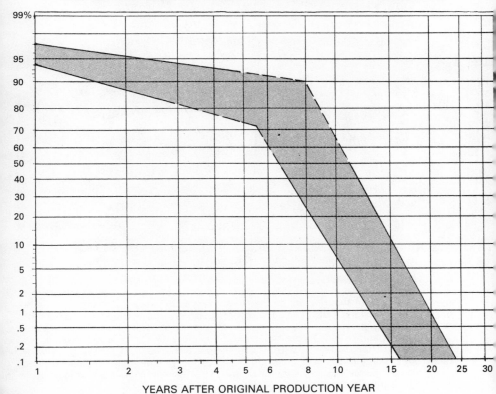

YEARS AFTER ORIGINAL PRODUCTION YEAR

more than twenty years old, may have survived to the tune of twenty percent of original production; but this is an exception.

Mr. Naul has checked a variety of makes and model years, and finds the graphs quite similar. Contrary to expectation, Cadillac cars disappear slightly faster than Chevrolets. Despite the theoretically larger budgets of luxury-car owners, the differences between makes are not great.

The big drop in survival after the sixth year is undoubtedly due to the cost of maintenance exceeding resale value. Without the sensible maintenance approach expressed earlier in this book, it's easy to see why so many owners see only one solution: trading in the old car for a newer one. Yet the rewards, for a smaller dollar investment, to owners willing to maintain their cars from the fifth through the tenth year, are sizeable, and they increase for each subsequent five-year period.

Owners of 1958 Chevrolets, of which 1,283,600 were built, can expect a registered ownership of only 1,284 in 1981. And demand for the 1958 model will exceed the supply, of that we can be sure.

The *Boston Sunday Globe* of June 3, 1973, carried an article about a Providence, Rhode Island, attorney who preferred to invest in cars rather than securities. He purchased a 1958 Lincoln Sedan with 34,000 miles for $2,100 at an auction in West Springfield, Massachusetts; and was quoted to the effect that it should be worth around $6,000 in five years. A look at auction prices, reported biweekly in *Old Cars* newspaper, suggests that there are quite a few such 'Rhode Island attorneys' around the country.

There is within the hobby, especially in England, a controversy about folks seeking only dollar appreciation vs. those sincerely interested in the charm of significant motorcars, whatever their sizes or values. I like the late Mort Kresteller's view best: One of the nation's leading collectors of pre-WW II cars, he was quoted in *Old Cars* newspaper:

This just has to be the greatest hobby. The guys you meet in car collecting are the nicest bunch you're going to find anywhere.

You want to know what I enjoy most about the hobby? No, it's not the shows. I enjoy the old style motoring, getting in the old cars, getting out on the back roads. It's a family affair. You take the wife and the kids, and everybody has a good time. You know, nowadays all the young people are taking drugs, getting high. I like to slow down, relax. I think that's what this hobby should be.

Look, the old man is home in the garage weekends working on the car. He's not on the golf course, with the old lady stuck home with the kids. When the car is finished everybody climbs in and away they go. Mom loves it. The kids love it. And when it comes time to sell the car you get every penny back. You might even make a couple of bucks. Now, where are you going to find a cheaper hobby, and have as much fun while you're at it? That's what I ask people. And they don't have the answer because in the long run there really isn't a cheaper hobby.[10]

Because scarcity and a car's charm are both important factors in defining 'collectibility,' convertibles may be your best bet. First, they tend to be used harder and are more vulnerable to the weather . . . thus they disappear faster. Result: faster recognition for the ones properly maintained. Second, convertible production has always been a low percentage of most manufacturers' total volume. Add to this Detroit's termination of new convertible production (the last American convertible was built in 1976 by Cadillac). Soon there will be

1957 CHRYSLER 300C CONVERTIBLE: One of 474 model 300 convertibles built in 1957. Horsepower had climbed to 390 at 5400 rpm . . . one horsepower for each of its 390 cubic inches. Compression ratio was 10:1. Suspension was by torsion bars. Acceleration from 0-60 mph was 8 seconds; top speed was 135+ mph. Wheelbase: 126 inches. A certified Milestone car.

CADILLAC ELDORADO CONVERTIBLE: The antithesis of good taste and design logic. For eleven years Cadillac fins had been growing and their overall length stretching; there seemed to be no end. Yet anyone who has traveled more than twenty miles in the back seat of these models knows the absurdity of its proportions — no more knee room than a compact Chevrolet Vega. Europeans called its grille the 'dollar grin.' This car was an example of the "conspicuous consumption" predicted by Thorstein Veblen in 1929. For these reasons, this was one of the most significant cars of the fifties. With entirely superfluous tail fins measuring forty-three inches from the ground in 1959, it was the epitome of indulgence in automobile design during the past quarter century. The car has an overall length of 225 inches. Wheelbase: 130 inches. Above is the 1954 model, below is the 1959. Lincoln and Imperial also achieved eight feet of body overhang during the late fifties.

nothing left but 'collector' convertibles, seen a few times a year in parades. Five or ten years from now, if you can gather the strength to sell, the charm of a convertible as an extra or family amusement car will surely get you extra dollars, all else being equal. Mercedes-Benz, Lincoln, Kaiser-Frazer — all have built highly-desirable four-door convertibles since WW II.

That's not to say that convertibles are the only premium body styles. The last twenty-five years have seen much innovation in body styling; not all of which reached high production. The most successful type is the pillarless two-door hardtop. Its acceptance has widened from its introduction in the forties into the seventies. Shorter-lived, and accordingly rarer, is the pillarless four-door hardtop.

THE PACKARD CARIBBEANS: Two fundamentally different Caribbeans were built between 1953 and 1956. Pictured is the second version, a dramatic V-8 with Torsion-Level Ride. In 1956 an electronic pushbutton transmission was standard (distinguished from Chrysler's mechanical version), as were reversible seat cushions: one side in leather, the other side a choice of fabrics. Horsepower of 290 hp and 310 hp were offered from a 374-cubic inch block. A 2.87:1 differential ratio was offered. Wheelbase for 1953-54: 122 inches; for 1955-56: 127 inches. The 1954 variation carried Packard's last straight-eight, a hearty 359-cubic inch engine that delivered 330 ft-lb of torque at 52 mph.

Still rarer are the pillarless four-door station wagons, though some of them had awkward styling.

Top-of-the line models should always be your first choice, as their difference in price compared to less stylish or elaborate models (between the fifth and tenth years, especially) is negligible, and usually they are rarer. Also, with the top model there usually comes a payload of accessories, which, while sometimes a pain in the neck, should not be shunned.

One of the differences between the pre-WW II enthusiast and the postwar (post-1950) enthusiast seems to be the latter's pro-

MERCEDES-BENZ 220S/SE CONVERTIBLE: Rudolf Uhlenhaut, the chief engineer of most post-WW II Mercedes-Benz cars, ranked the 220 engine (six-cylinder version) as one of his company's most significant achievements. In his judgment, this basic six-cylinder engine played a crucial role in the firm's recovery years. Simply stated, the motor worked well under adverse conditions throughout the world. The convertible and the coupe shared semi-handmade coachwork and body shells with the pre-1972 250, 280 and 300 coupes and convertibles. These cars have held their value exceedingly well; they wear out slowly, and their owners respect them sufficiently to take proper care of them. The fuel-injection version, first introduced in 1960, delivered one horsepower for each of its 134 cubic inches (2.2 liters). For all its luxury, the 220 had another charm — high gas mileage.

1951 CHRYSLER IMPERIAL: Conservative in appearance, this is among the most desirable of all Chryslers. It was the first year of the 180 hp 'hemi' V-8, and the last Imperial convertible for six years. Only 475 were built, and fewer than one dozen are known to survive today. Bodies and interiors by Briggs Body Company were extremely high in quality. Wheelbase: 131.5 inches.

1966 IMPERIAL CROWN CONVERTIBLE: The final year of the big open cars by Imperial was 1968. These stocky brutes may prove to be outstanding investments during the next few years. All large 1957-67 convertibles have not been saved as much as sports cars. With new cars getting smaller every year, these huge open models will be perceived very quickly as elegant giants. The engine was a 440-cubic inch V-8 with 480 ft-lb of torque at 2800 rpm. Wheelbase: 129 inches.

clivity for electronics. Electronic accessories came into their own in the early fifties. If half of these accessories don't work when you inspect a car, don't let that stop you; provided the body, interior, undercarriage and engine are in basically good condition. You may or may not seek to get every accessory functioning again, but having them is desirable. Often very minor problems prevent an accessory from working: nylon gears on power seats, pitted contact points on self-winding electric clocks, minor rust on electric window switches. New car dealers regrettably make mountains out of some of these repair molehills, and Detroit

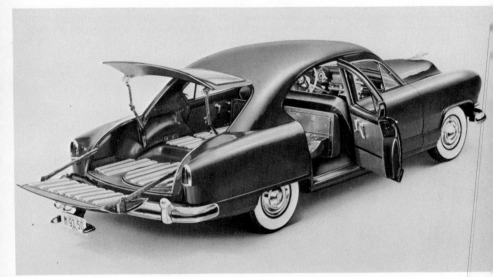

KAISER VAGABOND: First with many remarkable features, Kaiser and Frazer marketed a utility sedan from 1949 through 1953. The Traveler was built as a three-door model in 1949-50 ('51 for Frazer), and as two-door ('51) and four-door (1951-53) models by Kaiser. In the three-door model, the left rear door was fixed shut, with the spare tire just inside it. Styling of all Kaisers and Frazers is regarded as advanced and intelligent. The Kaiser-Frazer Clubs have a strong U.S. following. Wheelbase: 118.5 inches.

1940 FORD V-8 STATION WAGON: 'Woodies' and convertibles are the safest bets for reappreciation among old cars, assuming restoration is not too extensive. The true value of any car inherently includes the 'would-be' restoration cost to bring it to its original condition. If the wood on a station wagon is bad, the labor cost (if the owner is having it done) or the time cost (if the owner is doing it) for proper carpentry can be shocking. And no short-cuts are allowed: The right wood, correct joints and authentic wood staining are essential. Wood restoration results are more visible than any other type of restoration. All mechanical parts on these prewar Ford V-8's are easy to obtain. Nearly every part has been remanufactured and is available 'off the shelf' anywhere in the world.

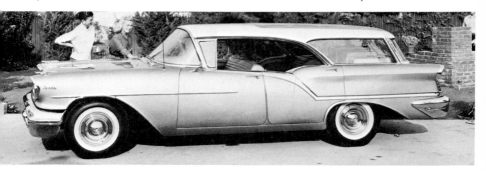

1957 OLDSMOBILE 88 FIESTA: A half-dozen manufacturers offered pillarless four-door wagons in the late fifties and early sixties, though precious few have been saved. This brings up the whole delightful history of station wagons, which could well become an area of specialization within the hobby. A collection of station wagons would start with a few of the fine, old 'woodies;' then the Willys 1946 steel-paneled station wagon or Plymouth's 1949 all-metal suburban wagon. After these pillarless four-door wagons, the 1960's brought us the Vista-Cruiser with a glass roof portion, and Studebaker's Wagonaire with a sliding roof section. All offered posh interior decors.

doesn't help. When I had my local Lincoln-Mercury dealer check the erratic power seat movements in an older Lincoln, they said new motors were required (both motors worked fine) "because Ford Motor Company does not sell the gears without motors." In other words, never do for $7.50 what you can do for $75. A fellow Lincoln owner I met two months later (I didn't buy the new motors) explained that only one of the gears breaks, and a replacement can be hand-crafted for less than $10. The point is, don't run away from unusual accessories, special body types or extinct makes. They will become scarce first, but also go up in value first.

Edsel is a realistic car to save for two reasons: Interchangeability of some parts with Fords and Mercurys, and Ford products have an unusually strong following among old-car buffs. Today, the Fords of the thirties bring two to ten times their originally-advertised prices.

Another bit of research by Marshall Naul concerns eighty-six new U.S. automobile makes introduced since 1945. Forty-two percent of all those new companies failed within one year. Ninety percent failed within six years.

Mr. Naul says, "The number of makes that 'fold' is nearly equal to those introduced, leaving a net gain of nearly zero. In short, the probability of success in the introduction of a new make in the U.S. market is quite small."[11] There are some delightful cars among those short-lived makes to which history will be very kind. The Edwards, an attractive fiberglass

1930 DUESENBERG MODEL J LE BARON PHAETON: From the Badenhausen Collection. Duesenberg phaetons are the reigning price giants of collector cars. In actual return on investment, however, they have not surpassed the 1934 Ford phaeton (below). The Ford sold new for less than $600 and now draws more than $12,000, or twenty-plus times its original cost. The Duesenberg phaetons sold new for an average of $16,000 and now command more than $200,000 . . . but that's not yet twenty times the original price. This model of the Duesenberg produced 265 hp at 4200 rpm. These fenders with the forked trim on the leading edge, a trademark, were designed for Duesenberg by 'Dutch' Darrin. Two wheelbases, 142.5 inches and 153.5 inches, were offered.

1934 FORD DELUXE PHAETON: A car with humble beginnings, it dramatizes the potential value of other cars in this book. Selling for $550 new in 1934, this 112-inch wheelbase, 85-hp flathead V-8 is worth more than twenty times that price today. A first-prize winner in its class at the 1973 Hershey Car Show and Swap Meet, it is owned by Robert Emery of Circle Pines, Minnesota. Mr. Emery owns an auto rebuilding firm called Restoration Enterprises, Inc. His Ford is particularly significant; it has the following now-rare accessories: firewall-mounted toolbox, ashtray radio, running board antenna, Columbia overdrive, bumper guards, fog lights, crank-hole cover, greyhound hood ornament, dual-temperature flash and gas gauge, dual-temperature flash amperage gauge and a luggage rack.

sports car built from 1953-55, with Lincoln engines, comes to mind. The Canadian-American Bricklin Company built only 2,610 units before its demise in 1975.

W. B. Hamlin of Ontario, California, has located fifty of the fifty-one Tucker cars built in 1948. These cars are dear, and when they do change hands the authentically-preserved cars easily command five-figure prices. As the years pass, they may prove to be the most valuable postwar motorcars built in the U.S.

Short-term vs. long-term return on investment is a consideration. Long-term — the special makes and body types will have the greatest appreciation. Despite this, a clean, plain sedan may be worth $1,000 more than a rusted prestige convertible, because restoration may cost two or three times the difference in initial purchase price on the rusty car. Short-term, you won't recover high restoration costs. Long-term, you will. Second-class restoration work (which is what two out of three shops offer) can never duplicate an original paint job, and often the third shop repaints too well, which is just as conspicuous as a poor job. Try to find matching upholstery for an interior; good upholsterers can be found, but the fabrics and leathers are hard to track down. (More on this later.) This is one reason to consider a newer (five to ten years old) car even though it will take a few years longer to appreciate. You'll have a greater choice of models, accessories and condition, and still end up with a mighty rare possession after a few years.

1947-48 TUCKER: Fifty-one of these ill-fated, highly-advanced cars were built. It is generally felt that Preston Tucker's scandal-laden enterprise was begun with the best intentions. But the project became too big for management's expertise, and dubious means were used in an unsuccessful attempt to bail out the Tucker. The car's engine is a marvel: A 334-cubic inch, six-cylinder, opposed rear engine that weighed only 320 lb, yet could propel the car faster than 100 mph and could exceed Oldsmobile's fast 88 series in acceleration. Numerous safety features included a center front light that turned with the front wheels. Prices today for the few authentically-preserved examples exceed $30,000. Beware, though, of substantially-modified engine swaps; quality of driving behavior varies considerably from car to car. Wheelbase: 130 inches.

FITCH-PHOENIX: Does that roof line look familiar? Like a 1972–75 Corvette? Guess again. It's an original design offered by Abercrombie & Fitch sporting goods stores in the early sixties! Designed by racing driver John Fitch (no relation), the car's body was assembled in Italy and a GM drive train was added under Mr. Fitch's direction after arrival in the USA. Cost new: $8,700. Wickedly beautiful and extremely rare.

BRICKLIN: Before this Canadian-American firm's demise in 1975, 2,610 Bricklins were built — an ideal number from a collector's standpoint. Ironically, the company's collapse enhances the car's collectibility. The Tucker's failure comes to mind; the personalities and sophisticated finances will surely provide material for an excellent book, as did Tucker. The Bricklin's AMC and Ford V-8 engines will help collectors in long-term preservation of these cars; however, the use of innovative but poorly formed body materials caused assembly problems that helped lead to the fatality of the company. Wheelbase: ninety-six inches. Height: forty-eight inches.

1955 GAYLORD: The 'flossy fifties' brought many dream cars into reality. If the Stutz Blackhawk was one of Virgil Exner's best efforts, this German Spohn-built Gaylord was among the finest designs to emerge from the Brooks Stevens staff. Financed by two brothers from Chicago, Ed and Jim Gaylord, the car was powered first by a supercharged Chrysler and later by a Cadillac engine. According to Gaylord the Chrysler was fastest, the Cadillac the smoothest and quietest. Serious production never got underway and pricing grew from an intended $10,000 each to $17,500. Many technical features were planned, including variable-ratio power steering and an automatically retractible hardtop. Wheelbase: one hundred inches.

6 Pick a Car That Suits You

Private enterprise has endowed the western world with a wide range of motorcar choices. Collectible cars abound, and more are discovered in barns and at estate sales every day. The best clearing-houses for locating and learning more about them are the four outstanding national publications listed below:

HEMMINGS
MOTOR NEWS
Box 380
Bennington, VT 05201
Monthly, $4.75
Ads only.
Circulation: 125,000

SPECIAL INTEREST
AUTOS
Box 7211
Stockton, CA 96207
Bi-monthly, $6 per yr.
Delightful historic articles
Circulation: 40,000

OLD CARS
Iola, WI 54945
26 issues per year, $6 per yr.
Newspaper format, hobby news, ads, and timely old car auction results. Outstanding.
Circulation: 75,000

CARS & PARTS
Box 299
Sesser, IL 62884
Articles and ads.
Monthly, $6 per yr.
Circulation: 75,000

These publications all have national circulation, and they provide the fastest way to become familiar with prices and types of cars available, even if you buy your first old car in your own neighborhood or state.

However, most important for your personal pleasure (which is very basic) is getting involved with vehicles that turn *you* on. Even you who are primarily interested in the investment opportunity must have a soft spot for some auto of the past.

When I was a boy my father owned a Pontiac 'Woodie' station wagon. It was a straight-eight Silver Streak model, and a fine vacation car indeed. It's strange what a gentle, but permanent, impression an experience like

1950 NASH RAMBLER: Updated by Pinin Farina for 1953-54. Models offered leather, dual-range Hydra-Matic drive, reclining seats and rare window railings over which the electrically-operated top was raised or lowered. Powered by an economical 183-cubic inch (three-liter) six-cylinder engine, twenty-gallon fuel tanks (and larger) were standard. Wheelbase: one hundred inches. There is a puzzling presence of small American cars throughout the post WW-II years: It cannot be said that Detroit ignored this segment of the market, or gave it to foreign manufacturers out of indifference.

that can leave with one. As a result, when I see a Pontiac straight-eight of any year (they were built up through 1954) I get melancholy. As I think about it today, any of the early Pontiac straight-eight Catalina two-door, pillarless hardtops (1950-52) would make distinctive and drivable cars to own. Eighty percent of these Catalina hardtops had full leather upholstery and hydramatic transmissions.

Or how about those delightful little Nash Rambler convertibles of the early fifties, with their permanent window frames over which the top descended? That was a safety-conscious design if ever there was one, and it's miserly gas consumption would also fit well into the seventies.

Which cars bring memories to you? Chances are a good specimen of your favorite is still to be found. Not in one month, but over the course of six months, just about anything will show up in those publications previously listed. Many of the friendliest people in the world are ready to help you for the modest cost of a club membership. The Milestone Car Society (MCS), about which more will follow, provides free research consultants on each certified Milestone car. Nearly every make of car also has what is called a single marque club concentrating on that make. Some of these single marque clubs have affiliated with MCS as the official register for that marque. Chapter 9 contains a list of many single marque clubs.

There are five basic functional types of cars which I'll take space here to review, as too few people give thought to the differences before purchase. Some people never do realize why they don't enjoy their cars; it may be they chose too large or too small a vehicle or one unusable in other ways.

Standard Cars (large, space no object). This includes any large sedan or station wagon capable of carrying at least five people and too much luggage. All power-assist equipment including air-conditioning is normally available. Soft ride and great comfort seem to be the main goals of this category: Examples include Ford Country Squire, Facel Vega Excellence, Imperial LeBaron, Oldsmobile Ninety-Eight, Chrysler New Yorker.

MERCEDES-BENZ 300SEL 6.3: With the same engine and suspension as the $25,000 Grand Mercedes 600, this utilitarian-looking motorcar will become an important collector's piece in years to come. From its first day of production this car was heralded as the world's greatest car. Indeed, this extended-wheelbase six-passenger auto will challenge and probably better the point-a-to-point-b elapsed time of any street-equipped sports car in the world. Quoting *Road and Track* magazine: "Its 6.3-liter V-8 gives acceleration of the Porsche, its air suspension gives a ride equal to the Jaguar XJ6 and the handling (at least in expert hands) is almost as good as that of the Ferrari 365 GTB/4. Yet it is the roomiest and most practical car. . ." Original price was $13,000 to $16,000. The 300SEL 6.3 is near its lowest point on the value curve at this time.

CADILLAC ELDORADO BROUGHAM: Cadillac probably tried harder to put all their know-how and accumulated technology into these models than into any other car they ever built. Anyone who has strived for perfection knows the law of diminishing returns: And Cadillac had its share of troubles with these complex autos; yet they rank among the greatest post-1945 cars. The notably condensed (1957-58) version suggested higher standards and more extensive thought than other larger Cadillacs. Among its features: ignition wired with rear door latches, air suspension, a 'memory' seat that 'remembered' several drivers' favorite sitting positions, three heaters, three-way rear-view mirror and Polaroid sun visors. Broughams in 1957-58 were built by Fleetwood, and were separate from regular Cadillacs. Severe domestic costs by 1958 caused the 1959-60 models to be sent out for assembly by Pinin Farina. Italian custom bodies (for all they are highly touted, in this book and elsewhere), have more than their share of body putty; paint crazing and cracking haunt the finest Ferraris, too. All Broughams had air suspension (Firestone), which has great historic value but parts replacement problems. Engines were standard Cadillac with extra carburetion. The top photo is of a 1957-58 Eldorado Brougham. Bottom photo: 1959-60 Eldorado Brougham.

Compact Cars. Common in Europe for many years, these cars have finally become popular in the U.S. They are shorter and make better use of space. While sizes fluctuate from make to make, performance and gas mileage differ much more. There is nothing wrong with that; there is certainly a demand for compact luxury cars with high performance. All Mercedes-Benz cars of the past ten years attest to this public demand and shatter the myth that quality comes only in a large package. The Buick Skylark series (1966-67) feel remarkably like their larger brothers, but are roughly a meter shorter. I can't understand why many people buy the larger Buicks when the slightly smaller model is available with the same accessories.

Compact cars have a long history in the U.S., but have not had much public acceptance until recently. An unusual collection would include examples of the various American efforts to introduce compact and sub-compact cars since 1935.

All of the following models are scarce and desirable today because few people have bothered to save them: original post-WW II Studebakers from 1947 through 1951, Kaiser's Henry J, the 1950-54 Rambler Convertible, the Willys Aero Eagle, England's Triumph Mayflower. You will probably think of three or four others.

Modern compacts include 1959-73 Rover three-liter, 1961-67 Oldsmobile F-85, 1961-67 Pontiac Tempest, Jaquar 3.8/4.2 Sedan and Citroen DS models.

Economy Cars/Mini Cars. In England there is a good deal of interest in preserving unusual small cars, the old three-wheel Morgan being a typical example. The Classic Car Club of America's orientation to cars costing more than $4,000 (when new) has inadvertently distracted collector attention (and funds) from preserving some of the most delightful small cars in the world. That is changing. The Messerschmitt (1952-53), the Playboy (1946-51), the Crosley Hotshot (1949-52), Honda S-600 (1962-64) are all rapidly becoming valuable. Economy cars are usually of simple, if unique, design, and they are relatively easy to understand and repair. They are quite realistic

FIAT 500 TOPOLINO: Fiat of Turin, Italy, was organized in 1899. Today it is one of Italy's largest employers, producing trucks, buses, tractors and home appliances, in addition to cars. Fiat sales have increased sharply in North America during the seventies, creating new interest in its early models. The Topolino was among Europe's quainter designs, along with Citroen's 2CV, the Volvo 544 and Volkswagen. Any of these cars can become permanent assets *and* outstanding local transportation vehicles.

as local, in-town transportation, though performance is measurable only in terms of low-speed handling and miles per gallon. Driving one in town can be a dickens of a lot of fun, and as a conversation piece it will match the finest Duesenberg. Other examples: Supera 360, BMW Isetta, Fiat Topolino, Vespa 400, NSU Wankel Spyder and Citroen 2CV.

Personal Cars. This group of non-sports cars is designed specifically for driver convenience. They have shorter wheelbases and bodies than sedans; consequently they handle better. The personal car, or 'gran turismo' (grand touring) as it is called in Europe, is a high-speed, cross-country touring car, as distinguished from normal touring se-

JENSEN INTERCEPTOR III: On the road, the Jensen seemed to take up where the Citroen SM left off. The Jensen was a fine turnpike adventurer, though its suspension was not as versatile as the SM's on rough or mountainous roads. The Type II Jensen substantially outperformed the Type III in acceleration and gas mileage. Type II: 383-cubic inch Chrysler V-8 engine, 0-60 mph in 7.4 seconds with average gas mileage of 14 mpg. Type III: 440-cubic inch Chrysler V-8 engine, 0-60 mph in 10.4 seconds and average gas mileage of 11 mpg. Wheelbase: 105 inches. The history of the British-built Jensens, through its recent American ownership, can be found in *The Jensen Healey Stories*, by Browning and Blunsden.

dans. It is limited to two doors, though most have a back seat. Personal cars are generally good performers, and offer a choice of engines. They offer better weather protection than sports cars.

Recent examples include: 1964-73 Ford Mustang, Avanti I and II, 1972-73 Jensen Interceptor, 1955-73 Karmann Ghia, Chevrolet Camero.

The Oldsmobile Toronado, Buick Riviera and Continental II, III and IV, while

AVANTI: Like proud parents, Studebaker president Sherwood Egbert and Raymond Loewey stand by Studebaker's final wonder. Even a prototype four-door version was built before the end. Most original Avanti production occurred in 1963; a few square headlight versions were run in 1964. Total 1963–64 production was 4,643. The early Avanti was an earthy machine: fast, stiff-riding and noisy. The public loved it. Good examples of the Avanti command higher prices today than when they were new. Avanti II came about after the Avanti body toolings were purchased from Studebaker by Nate Altman and Leo Newman of South Bend; hand-built cars with GM ohv V-8 engines emerged. Avanti II was a vehicle with much more civilized insulation, vibration dampening, craftsmanship and accessory options. Used Avanti II's deserve a close look. Wheelbase: 109 inches.

1968 AMX: This is one of a number of American Motors cars destined for recognition. A national AMX owners' club already exists, and many owners chastized me for not including a photo of the AMX in my first edition of this book. An atypical American personal car, the AMX offered special handling items, including rear traction-bars, large-diameter front sway bar, heavy-duty springs and shocks and belted wide-profile tires. Three V-8 engine choices were available, all with four-barrel carburetion. They included the standard 290-cubic inch V-8 and optional 343-cubic inch and 390-cubic inch V-8's.

BMW 507: Offered during the fifties, Germany's 507 arouses that keen sense of pleasure we call beauty as well as any motor car that ever touched the ground. The body design is attributed to Albrecht Goertz of New York. With a V-8 engine of slightly more than 190 cubic inches (three liters), it generated 173 horses, which in turn provided a 134-mph top speed. A soft top and removable hardtop were available.

rather personal in styling and features, are too large to qualify as personal cars. I would put them in a category of passenger cars pretending to be personal cars.

Sports Cars. Sporting cars are usually broken into two subgroups, road cars and track machines. Some are more easily distinguished than others. The Sports Car Club of America used to require: four fenders fastened to the body, brake lights and headlights, only two doors, only two seats but not less, a self-starter, spare tire, etc. Quick inspection of a sports car will show if it was equipped to win races or to drive on public streets. Some manufacturers offer one ideal model intended for both road and track. Not many really succeed, but these models are desirable historically. Below are

1959-1964 ALFA ROMEO: Giulietta Sprint with Speciale body by Carrozzeria Bertone. She's 'speciale' whatever her name is! Italy's answer to the Karmann Ghia was another custom body with economical, standard drive train: A certified Milestone with a tiny, eighty-cubic inch (1300 cc) engine producing 100 hp, a 125 mph top speed and twenty-five miles per gallon of gas! Formed in 1906, Alfa has always been known for precise, feather-light handling — without power steering! The Speciale's wheelbase was eighty-nine inches. Beware of terminal rust on the unit body and suspension points of this particular model. But if you find a good Speciale it will compare with a delicate vintage wine.

PORSCHE 356 CABRIOLET: A recent issue of *Autoweek* reported that George Frey's fifteen-year-old Porsche Speedster broke an existing class racing record competing against brand new cars. Porsche defied the conventional wisdom of 'no substitute for cubic inches.' The result has been one of the finest racing histories in motordom. The original Speedsters cost only $3,500 new, and they sell for well above that figure today. The Cabriolet brought an elegance to hair-raising motoring that almost made it seem proper. Wheelbase: eighty-three inches. Top photo is a 356 Speedster in action.

some sports cars in their generally accepted subgroups.

Public Road Sports Cars
    Porche 356, 911 and 912
    Fiat 1200 TV and 124
    BMW 507
    Mercedes-Benz 230SL through 300SL
Ideal Sports Cars
    Alfa Romeo Guilietta
    Fiat Abarth
    Porsche Carrara
    Ferrari 250 GT Berlinetta
Sports Racing Cars
    Lister Jaguar
    Lotus 1600
    Osca 750
    Cooper Climax

Keep your actual car uses in mind, and you will find yourself more frequently using and enjoying your 'new' motorcar as well as regarding it as a good investment.

1953-54 KAISER DARRIN 161: One of the giants of tasteful automobile designing for six decades has been Howard 'Dutch' Darrin. You can still commission Dutch to tailor a car for you — one, or 100,000. From Duesenberg's fender line to Frazer Manhattans and Packard Victorias, Darrin's contributions have always been original and elegant. A total of 497 Darrin 161 Deauville convertibles were built, with unique sliding doors and fiberglass bodies. More than two hundred of these cars have survived, but very few change hands each year.

7 Exotic Cars

And now to those mystical machines that few of us will ever be able to afford, from the houses of Ferrari, Rolls Royce, Facel Vega and the like. The subject of investing in cars wouldn't be complete without discussing exotic cars, as they will be the first to reach ultra-high reappreciation levels as they settle into distinguished old age.

Auction prices for rare-bodied, pre-WW II Mercedes-Benz', Duesenbergs and Bugattis *regularly* exceed $100,000. While this is enough to make anyone blink, I can tell you firsthand that cars with this potential come with maintenance bills of commensurate size. There are always lucky exceptions, but I'll go out on a limb and say that for any exotic car that is regularly driven 7,500 miles per year and more, one can expect that sooner or later the average annual maintenance (excluding gas, oil and depreciation) will reach ten percent of the original purchase price — that is, ten percent per year! A $3,000 car will cost $300 per year to keep up. Some years the owner will get by for $100, others, $500. A $30,000 Ferrari, if

1954 FERRARI 375: Powered by a 229-cubic inch engine; capable of 185 mph at 6800 to 7000 rpm; 0-60 mph in 6.5 seconds; five-speed transmission; 102-inch wheelbase. Prior to 1955, standardized bodies were unknown at Ferrari. This Pinin Farina design predated Chrysler's wraparound windshield treatment, and looks very modern to an average 'car spotter,' even today. Hard to believe she's twenty years old. A large variety of Ferrari chassis and body choices are available to the collector; some early four- and six-cylinder models are still around.

LAMBORGHINI ESPADA: Almost a four-passenger vehicle, at about $6,000 per passenger. These wonderful-looking cars are shaky investments; parts and service are both extremely scarce and astronomically expensive. Its V-12 engine produced 350 hp. Wheelbase: 104 inches.

BENTLEY: The Rolls-Royce firm has a few standard bodies, all fairly popular, though you can rely on finding a soft spot in each Manchester connoisseur's heart for the custom bodies by any of a half-dozen builders. One of the best is this (by Pininfarina again), the Bentley T, created in 1968. Wheelbase: 120 inches; powered by an aluminum V-8 engine.

1960 ROLLS-ROYCE: The Phantom V, a 144-inch wheelbase model, has a 380-cubic inch (6.2-liter) V-8 engine. Built to last, quality of maintenance is the largest determinant of future value. Typical examples sell for $30,000-plus and are worth every cent from a stability-of-investment standpoint. Limousines generally are soft investments, especially Cadillacs, because there are too many built each year for collector appeal. Low-production years and rare body variations are the most desirable.

driven regularly and kept in prime condition, will approach $3,000 annually for maintenance — not the first year, but as an average. Many owners will say they don't spend anywhere near that percentage; but then they may not be amortizing their forthcoming engine-rebuilding jobs or they may be running their cars into the ground.

The point is, the big-dollar exotic cars are kings' playthings (or kings' works of art, in some cases); and a very fine example draws a very fine price because buyers know what it costs in time and money to return a marginal one to top condition.

A colorful history, such as a car's having had famous past owners, will usually sweeten the coffers at resale time, as will special coachwork by established body builders.

LOTUS ELITE II: Brilliant, far-sighted designing causes certain cars to stay in the limelight for decades and decades. Of the mid-seventies motorcars, which are 'the fairest of them all'? I suspect that elements of this four-seater's shape will be with us well into the 1990's. The need for rear-seat head-room is nicely served by the 'wedge-shape' and 'portwagon' concepts. Applied to this Elite II, the result is a four-passenger sports car compact enough to deliver twenty-five miles per gallon, exceed 125 mph and meet or surpass all federal emission and safety standards. This is a conventional front engine, rear-wheel drive layout. Wheelbase: 97.7 inches.

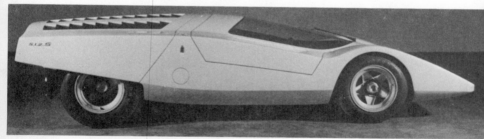

FERRARI 512 S BERLINETTA SPECIALE: The Speciale had a rear-mounted twelve-cylinder engine of 304 cubic inches and 500 horsepower at 8000 rpm, hemispherical combustion chambers, seven main bearings and fuel injection. A five-speed fully-synchronized transmission, limited slip-differential, light-alloy tubular frame and independent suspension were offered. Overall height was 38.6 inches (four inches lower than the '59 Eldorado fins). Pininfarina and other body builders in recent years have put considerable thought into the wedge shape shown here. You've seen a taste of it in Ford's much-publicized de Tomaso Pantera, and several four-passenger exotics, including the Lotus Elite II and the Karmann/Ital design called 'Ace of Clubs.' With Ferrari, Pininfarina, Ford, de Tomaso, Vignale, Bertone and three or four other concerns all on the same path, a significant trend is inevitably in the making. Interior accommodations on this Speciale were every bit as creative as the exteriors, and more comfortable than they might appear. Wheelbase: 94.5 inches.

8 This Business of Size and Quality

The U.S.A.'s little Rambler American has a bigger engine than one of Europe's biggest and most expensive automobiles. The foreign make has half again the weight and it completely outperforms its American counterpart.

	Engine Size	Weight	0-60 mph Acceleration	Top Speed
1960-62 Rambler American	6 cyl 195 cu	2,600 lb	16 sec	86 mph
1960-62 Mercedes-Benz 300	6 cyl 183 cu	4,500 lb	13.5 sec	100 mph

For many years Rolls-Royce's standard sedan, the Silver Cloud, was equipped with a six-cylinder engine thirty percent smaller than the American Lincoln's engine. Yet the Rolls-Royce cost twice as much. What's the conclusion? An engine's quality is not determined by its size, or by which car it is mounted in. It's the performance that counts: speed, safety, comfort, handling, economy, etc. (in the first example we must grant the Rambler about a five mpg advantage over the Mercedes).

Neither engine size, body size, length or price can be considered an accurate measure of an automobile's quality or performance ability. Quality goes deeper than physical dimensions.

The same rule applies to riding qualities. The compact Citroen provides one of the world's smoothest rides, yet its overall length is only 189 inches, more than a yard shorter than the Buick Electra.

These are a few of the reasons for not generalizing that *large* cars are quality cars and *small* cars are of poorer quality.

Price is also sometimes a poor measure of quality. It is usually assumed that an $8,500 automobile has more quality than a $5,500 automobile. But such is not always the case.

First, we should agree on what 'quality' means. Power steering, automatic transmission and air conditioning do not constitute 'quality.' These items are accessories which contribute to greater convenience, or luxury, while driving. Luxury is not quality; quality is a luxury. Quality is good craftsmanship: precision manufacture *and* precision assembly of all parts. An Oldsmobile or Buick, fully equipped with accessories, sells for $8,000 or more. They are large cars even by American standards. A Saab selling for $5,500-$6,000 contains as much or more 'quality' as $8,500 Buicks and Oldsmobiles.

9 Enthusiasts' Subculture

I have stopped being amazed at the following that emerges for every marque and automobile model built! You name it — even the most homely, under-engineered model of them all — and there are some people still driving the cars, regardless of how old they are. The same is true of parts sources. Often retired people and ex-dealers with detailed firsthand knowledge of a make will single out a few years or models and preserve a significant parts source for them. It's not too hard to become the expert if one limits his years of concentration. Nearly every state has some high-caliber sales and service centers specializing in pre-1965 cars (see Chapter 14).

An important role is performed by national car clubs that put owners in touch with key sources for replacement parts. Once a few good sources are located, it's a perfunctory matter to get the parts. At first a new owner may be overly concerned about the potential scarcity of his car, and he contemplates buying a similar model strictly for use as a parts source. If you last a year without acquiring one, you will have come across so many leads on parts that you may never bother with a 'parts' car. That's not to say it's a bad idea, but unless you know of a shed you can rent for next to nothing, don't bother. Unused parts cars sitting behind your garage just get the neighbors angry. Since buying my 1954 Lincoln, I have learned of one man with four similar parts cars, and another man near St. Louis with twenty-five! Same story with my 1948 Jeepster; thanks to the Mid-States Jeepster Club, I located a gentleman in New Jersey who owns more than twenty-five Jeepster parts cars and makes a business of supplying 1948-51 Jeepster owners. This is typical, and both the Lincoln and Jeepster are fairly rare now. You will find suppliers for the newer and higher-

1946 WILLYS STATION WAGON: World's first production 'all-steel' wagon, this model was built into the early fifties, with minor modifications. Willys-Overland expected a big post-WW II market among veterans for a civilian vehicle with a Jeep-like appearance, both in the wagon and in the Jeepster. The market did not prove to be significant, though four-wheel drive wagons, pick-ups and panel Willys have been owned by nearly every gasoline service station in the country, at one time or another.

production models in every state and province.

The clubs are a real asset, even if you seek technical information more than social contacts (though I have found the two mix nicely). Since they don't get published very often, here is a list of auto enthusiast clubs. Don't hesitate to contact these organizations before you buy; many of them have 'wanted' and 'for sale' columns in their membership newsletters. Most allow membership without car ownership, so you can read their publications and attend their events prior to buying. This quite comprehensive list was compiled by *Old Cars* newspaper. These addresses may change, but even so I suspect your inquiries will be forwarded.

WILLYS JEEPSTER: A surprise reception was given the Willys Jeepster by the Milestone Car Society's (MCS) prestigious nominations committee; all eleven advisors declared the Jeepster worthy of Milestone status. Criteria were styling, performance and innovativeness; shown is the 1950-51. Both cars had their own advantages: The earlier cars had pleated upholstery, rear fender step-plates and more trim; the later cars employed overhead valve four- and six-cylinder engines and V-shaped grilles. Both had uncommonly substantial X-frames not shared by any other Willys vehicle. Total 1948-51 production. 19,131. Wheelbase: 104 inches. An active register of Jeepster owners is affiliated with the MCS.

Multi-Make Organizations

ANTIQUE AUTOMOBILE CLUB OF AMERICA, 501 W. Governor Rd., Hershey, PA 17033.

ANTIQUE AND CLASSIC CAR CLUB OF CANADA, Box 1304, Postal Station A, Toronto, Ontario, M5W 1G7, Canada.

CLUB MEXICANO DE AUTOMOBILES ANTIQUES A.C., P.O. Box 20-020, Mexico 20.

D.F. HISTORICAL AUTOMOBILE SOCIETY OF CANADA, 23 Maple Drive, Orrillia, Ontario, Canada.

HORSELESS CARRIAGE CLUB OF AMERICA. 9031 E. Florence Ave., Arrington Square, Downey, CA 90240.

MID-AMERICA OLD TIME AUTOMOBILE ASSOCIATION, 1799 Mignon, Memphis, TN 38107.

PIONEER AUTOMOBILE TOURING CLUB, 252 North 7th St., Allentown, PA 18102.

STEAM AUTOMOBILE CLUB OF AMERICA, 333 N. Michigan Ave., Chicago, IL 60601.

VEHICLE RESTORERS ASSOC., Box 761, Regina, Sask., 54P 3A8, Canada.

VETERAN MOTOR CAR CLUB OF AMERICA, 105 Elm St., Andover, MA 01810.

VINTAGE CAR CLUB OF CANADA, Box 3070, Vancouver, B.C., Canada.

CLASSIC CAR CLUB OF AMERICA, Box 443, Madison, NJ 07940.

LE CERCLE CONCOURS D'ELEGANCE, 9476 Readcrest Drive, Beverly Hills, CA 90210.

CONTEMPORARY HISTORICAL VEHICLE ASSOCIATION, 1124 W. Fern Drive, Fullerton, CA 92633.

THE MILESTONE CAR SOCIETY, Box 1166Z, Pacific Palisades, CA 90272.

ANTIQUE TRUCK CLUB OF AMERICA, 8-19 115th St., College Point, NY 11356.

INTERNATIONAL TRUCK RESTORERS ASSOC., 2026 Bayer Ave., Fort Wayne, IN 46805.

MOTOR BUS SOCIETY, 767 Valley Road, Upper Montclair, NJ 07043.

SEDAN DELIVERIES LIMITED, 48 Church St., Slatersville, RI 02876.

SOCIETY FOR THE PRESERVATION AND APPRECIATION OF ANTIQUE MOTOR FIRE APPARATUS IN AMERICA. Box 450, Eastwood Station, Syracuse, N.Y. 13206.

NATIONAL MILITARY VEHICLE COLLECTORS ASSOC., Box 23491, Los Angeles, CA 90023.

SPORTS CAR COLLECTORS SOCIETY, Box 1855, Quantico, VA 22134.

VINTAGE SPORTS CAR CLUB, 2035 Greenwood, Wilmette, IL 60091.

VINTAGE SPORTS CAR CLUB OF AMERICA, 170 Wetherill Rd., Garden City, NY 11530.

NATIONAL WOODY CLUB, 5522 West 140th St., Hawthorne, MA 90250.

Special Purpose Organizations

AUTO ENTHUSIASTS INTERNATIONAL, Box 2379, Dearborn, MI 48123.

AUTOMOTIVE POSTCARD COLLECTORS CLUB, 155 Tamarack Dr., Rochester, NY 14622.

MADISON AVENUE SPORTS CAR DRIVING AND CHOWDER SOCIETY, 10 Holder Place, Forest Hills, NY 11375.

SOCIETY OF AUTOMOTIVE HISTORIANS, Stublyn Rd., Rte. 2, Granville, OH 43023.

Single Marque Clubs

THE AC OWNERS CLUB, American Centre, 88 Cushing Street, Hingham, MA 02043.

AHRENS-FOX FIRE BUFFS ASSOCIATION, Box 233, Rte. 2, Schwenksville, PA 19473.

ALFA-ROMEO OWNERS CLUB, Box 331, Northbrook, IL 60062.

ALLARD OWNERS CLUB U.S.A., 33 Lenderwood Rd., Montville, N.J. 07045.

THE ALLARD REGISTER, 8 Paget Close, Horsham, West Sussex RH13 6HD, England.

THE ALVIS OWNERS CLUB, No. American Section, Box 768, Milford, PA 18337.

AMERICAN AUSTIN-BANTAM CLUB, Box 328, Morris, NY 13808.

CLASSIC AMX CLUB, 220 West Renrose Ave., Loves Park, IL 61111.

THE AMILCAR REGISTER, 27 Farnborough Crescent, Addington, Surrey, England.

THE ARMSTRONG-SIDDELEY OWNERS CLUB LTD., 90 Alumhurst Rd., Westbourne, Bournemouth, Dorset, England.

ARNOLT-BRISTOL REGIS-TRY, 9382 Gina Drive, West Chester, OH 45069.

ASTON-MARTIN OWNERS CLUB, U.S.A. Centre, 195 Mount Paran Rd. NW, Atlanta, GA 30327.

AUBURN-CORD-DUESENBERG CLUB, Box 11635, Palo Alto, CA 94306.

AUSTIN SEVEN CLUB, 65 Hornby Ave., Southend-on-Sea, Essex, England.

VINTAGE AUSTIN REGISTER, 17 Grove Park Ave., Sittingbourne, Kent, England.

AUSTIN-HEALEY CLUB, P.O. Box 6267, San Jose, CA 95150.

BENTLEY DRIVERS CLUB, LTD., 16 Chearsley Rd., Long Crendon, Bucks, England.

BMW CAR CLUB OF AMERICA, Vintage/Classic Division, 2 Brewster, Cambridge, MA 02138.

BMW 507 OWNERS CLUB U.S.A. c/o Barry McMillan, Hilltown Pike, Hilltown, PA 18927.

BMW AUTOMOBILE CLUB OF AMERICA, P.O. Box 401, Hollywood, CA 90028.

VINTAGE/CLASSIC DIVISION, BMW CAR CLUB OF AMERICA, 2 Brewer St., Cambridge, MA 02138.

BROUGH SUPERIOR CLUB, 184 Saffron Lane, Leicester, England.

AMERICAN BUGATTI CLUB, Box 263, South Laguna, CA 92677.

BUICK CLUB OF AMERICA, Box 853, Garden Grove, CA 92642.

McLAUGHLIN-BUICK CLUB OF CANADA, 99 Simcoe St., Oshawa, Ontario, Canada.

CADILLAC-LASALLE CLUB, 3340 Poplar Dr., Warren, MI 48020.

SPECIAL INTEREST CADILLACS, 21606 Bayside, St. Clair Shores, MI 48081.

CHEVROLET REGISTER-1941, 6528 South Main, Anderson, IN 46013.

CLASSIC CHEVROLET CLUB, Rt. 4, 58 Mineola Dr., New Port Richey, FL 33552.

NATIONAL CHEVROLET RESTORERS CLUB, Box 311, LaMirada, CA 90637.

NATIONAL NOMAD CLUB, 50 Teller St., Lakewood, CO 80226.

VINTAGE CHEVROLET CLUB OF AMERICA, Box 1135, Bellflower, CA 90706.

AIRFLOW CLUB OF AMERICA, 2029 Minoru Drive Altadena, CA 91001.

CHRYSLER 300 CLUB, Box 264, Northridge, CA 91324.

CHRYSLER 300 CLUB, EASTERN DIVISION, 3033 Curran Rd. Louisville, KY 40205.

TOWN & COUNTRY OWNERS REGISTRY, R.D. 1, Box 841, Orefield, PA 18069.

GOLDEN LIONS, 909 Edgewood Terrace, Wilmington, DE 19809.

WALTER P. CHRYSLER CLUB INC., 17916 Trenton Drive, Castro Valley, CA 94546.

WALTER P. CHRYSLER CLUB, EASTERN DIVISION, 5986 Irishtown Rd., Bethel Park, PA 15102.

CITROEN CAR CLUB, Box 743, Hollywood, CA 90028.

CORVAIR SOCIETY OF AMERICA, 145 Ivywood St., Radnor, PA 19087.

NATIONAL COUNCIL OF CORVETTE CLUBS, 3044 W. Grand Blvd., Detroit, MI 48202.

VINTAGE CORVETTE CLUB OF AMERICA, 2359 W. Adams, Fresno, CA 93706.

CROSLEY AUTOMOBILE CLUB, 200 Ridge Rd. East, Williamson, NY 14589.

DAIMLER & LANCHESTER OWNERS' CLUB, 1 Lullington Road Overseal, Burton-on-Trent, Staffordshire, England.

D.B. AND PANHARD REGISTRY, 23 Clyde St., Buffalo, NY 14215.

DATSUN Z CLUB OF AMERICA, 124 Getty Ave., Clifton, NJ 07011.

LES AMIS DE DELAGE, Siege Social et Secretariat, Chateau des Ducs de Bretagne, 44-Nantes, France.

DELAHAYE CLUB, c/o Jean Pierre Bernard, Les Milans, La Celle, St. Cloud, France.

DE SOTO CLUB OF AMERICA, 105 E. 96th St., Kansas City, MO 64114.

DODGE EIGHT AUTOMOTIVE REGISTRY, Box 165, Kearny, NJ 07032.

DURANT OWNERS CLUB, 3106 Plymouth Rock Rd., Norristown, PA 19403.

EDSEL OWNERS CLUB OF AMERICA, Box 7, West Liberty, IL 62475.

INTERNATIONAL EDSEL CLUB, Box 304, Bellevue, OH 44811.

ERSKINE REGISTER, 441 East St., Almont, MI 48003.

FACEL VEGA CLUB, Box 295, Novi, MI 48050.

FERRARI CLUB OF AMERICA, 5908 W. 41st Ave. Gary, IN 46408.

FIAT CLUB OF AMERICA, Box 192, Somerville, MA 02143.

EARLY FORD V-8 CLUB OF AMERICA, Box 2122, San Leandro, CA 94577.

FABULOUS FIFTIES FORD CLUB OF AMERICA, Box 2102, Canoga Park, CA 91306.

FORD AND MERCURY CLUB OF AMERICA, Box 3551, Hayward, CA 94540.

FORD AND MERCURY RESTORERS CLUB, Box 2133, Dearborn, MI 48125.

FORTIES LIMITED, 16752 Huggins Ave., Yorba Linda, CA 92686.

MODEL A FORD CLUB OF AMERICA. P.O. Box 1791, Whittier, CA 90603.

MODEL A RESTORERS CLUB, Box 1930A, Dearborn, MI 48123.

MODEL T FORD CLUB INTERNATIONAL, P.O. Box 915, Elgin, IL 60120.

MODEL T FORD CLUB OF AMERICA, Box 711, Oceanside, CA 92054.

MUSTANG OWNERS CLUB, 115 Fairmont St., Malden, MA 02148.

NATIONAL CROWN VICTORIA ASSOC. 831½ No. Jefferson, St., Muncie, IN 47303.

RETRACTABLE FORD CLUB, c/o Toby Gorney, Rte. 5, Spring Valley Estates, Bryan, OH 43506.

SHELBY OWNERS ASSOCIATION, 28 Union Ave., Hempstead, NY 11550.

TWO CYLINDER FORD REGISTER, 9734 Garnish St., Downey, CA 90240.

H. H. FRANKLIN CLUB, c/o Cazenovia, NY 13035.

FRAZER-NASH SECTION OF THE VINTAGE SPORTS CAR CLUB, 65 Coventry St., Kidderminster, Worcs, DY10 2BS, England.

GENERAL MOTORS RESTORERS CLUB, Box 143, Highland Station, Springfield, MA 01109.

GRAHAM OWNERS CLUB INTERNATIONAL, Box 105, Burlington, MA 01803.

HAYNES AND APPERSON OWNERS CLUB, 409 E. Walnut St., Kokomo, IN 46901.

HILLMAN REGISTER 73 Church Rd., Wimbledon, London SW 19, England.

HISPANO-SUIZA SOCIETY OF AMERICA, 230 Park Ave., New York, NY 10017.

HUDSON ESSEX TERRAPLANE CLUB, 23104 Dolorosa St., Woodland Hills, CA 91364.

HUMBER REGISTER, Angel Road, Thames Dilton, Surrey, England.

HUPMOBILE CLUB, Box AA, Rosemead, CA 91770.

ISOTTA-FRASCHINI OWNERS ASSOCIATION, 9704 Illinois St., Hebron, IL 60034.

CLASSIC JAGUAR ASSOCIATION, Snedens Landing, Palisades, NY 10964.

JAGUAR AFFILIATES GROUP, 23713 Glenbrook, St: Clair Shores, MI 48082.

JAGUAR OWNERS CLUB, 1733 N. San Antonio Ave., Upland, CA 91786.

MIDSTATES JEEPSTER ASSOCIATION, c/o Thomas Adams, 16 Hopewell Hills, Lacon, IL 61540.

WILLYS OVERLAND JEEPSTER CLUB, 395 Dumbarton Blvd., Cleveland, OH 44143.

JOWETTE CAR CLUB, "The Briars," Castledon Rd., Downham, Billericay, CM11 1LH, England.

KAISER-FRAZER OWNERS CLUB, 705 No. Lillian St., McHenry, IL 60050.

KISSEL KAR KLUB, RD 2, Box 92A, Hartford, WI 53027.

THE LAGONDA CLUB, 10 Crestwood Trail, Lake Mohawk, Sparta, NJ 07871.

LAMBORGHINI CLUB OF AMERICA, c/o G.T. Cars, 3054 N. Lake Terrace, Glenview, IL 60025.

AMERICAN LANCIA CLUB, 50 Mansion Rd., Springfield, PA 19064.

LEA-FRANCIS OWNERS CLUB, c/o J. T. Woodhouse, Esq., "Milestone," 105 Boxley Dr., West Bridgeford, Nottingham NG2 76N, England.

LINCOLN CONTINENTAL OWNERS CLUB, Box 549, Nogales, AZ 85621.

LINCOLN OWNERS CLUB, 9821 Copper Hill Rd., St. Louis, MO 63124.

LINCOLN ZEPHYR OWNERS CLUB, Box 185, Middletown, PA 17057.

ROAD RACE LINCOLN REGISTER, 41 Musket Trail, Simsbury, CT 06070.

THE 1956-57 LINCOLN PREMIERE REGISTRY, 192 Arnoldale Rd., West Hartford, CT 06119.

CLUB ELITE, Box 351, Clarksville, TN 37040.

LOTUS WEST, Box 75972, Los Angeles, CA 90005.

MARMON REGISTER, 5364 Stuart Ave. S.E., Grand Rapids, MI 49508.

GULL WING GROUP, Box 2093, Sunnyvale, CA 94087.

MERCEDES-BENZ CLUB OF AMERICA, Box 2183, Sunnyvale, CA 94087.

MERCER ASSOCIATES, Dept. of Business Administration, Texas Tech, Lubbock, TX 79409.

HEINKEL - MESSERSCHMITT - ISETTA CLUB, P. O. Box 90, Topanga, CA 90290.

MESSERSCHMITT OWNERS CLUB, USA, 39 Sylvan Way, West Caldwell, NJ 07006.

METZ REGISTER. c/o Franklin B. Tucker, 216 Central Ave., West Caldwell, NJ 07006.

CLASSIC M.G. CLUB, 1307 Ridgecrest Rd., Orlando, FL 32806.

NEW ENGLAND M.G. "T" REGISTER, Drawer 220, Oneonta, NY 13820.

MONTIVERDI OWNERS OF AMERICA, Suite 1201, 575 Park Ave., New York, NY 10017.

MORGAN CAR CLUB OF WASHINGTON, D.C., 616 Gist Avenue, Silver Spring, MD 20910.

MORGAN OWNERS GROUP, 40-01 Little Neck Pkwy., Little Neck, NY 11362.

MORGAN PLUS FOUR CLUB, 5073 Melbourne Drive, Cypress, CA 90630.

MORGAN THREE WHEELER CLUB, U.S. GROUP, 1051 16th St. Santa Monica, CA 90403.

LAFAYETTE OWNERS CLUB OF AMERICA, 176½ East 75th St., New York, NY 10021.

METROPOLITAN OWNERS CLUB, 839 W. Race St., Somerset, PA 15501.

MINI OWNERS OF AMERICA, Box 2872-D, Pasadena, CA 91105.

NASH CAR CLUB OF AMERICA, R. R. 1, Clinton, IA 52732.

NASH HEALEY CAR CLUB INTERNATIONAL, RD. 1 Lakeshore Drive, Addison, PA 15411.

NSU ENTHUSIASTS USA, RD No. 2, Corning, NY 14830.

CURVED DASH OLDS OWNERS CLUB, 7 Kiltie Dr., New Hope, PA 18938.

OLDSMOBILE CLUB OF AMERICA, Box 1498, Samp Motar Sta., Fairfield, CT 06430.

OLDSMOBILE CLUB OF CANADA, 117 Hespeler Ave., Winnipeg, Man. Canada R2L 0L5.

PACKARD AUTOMOBILE CLASSICS, Box 2808, Oakland, CA 94618.

PACKARDS INTERNATIONAL MOTOR CAR CLUB, 302 French St., Santa Ana, CA 92701.

PIERCE-ARROW SOCIETY, 135 Edgerton St., Rochester, NY 14607.

PLYMOUTH 4 & 6 CYLINDER OWNERS CLUB, 300 E. 12th St. Fremont, NE 68025.

PLYMOUTH SUPERBIRD CLUB, 43 Greeley St., Tiffin, OH 44883.

NATIONAL BARRACUDA OWNERS CLUB, PO Box 478, Detroit, MI 48232.

PONTIAC-OAKLAND CLUB INTERNATIONAL, 3298 Maple Ave., Allegany, NY 14706.

SAFARI CLUB OF AMERICA, 220 17th Ave. So., Seattle, WA 98144.

OAKLAND-PONTIAC ENTHUSIASTS ORGANIZATION, Box 518, Keego Harbor, MI 48033.

PORSCHE CLUB OF AMERICA, 5616 Clermont Dr., Alexandria, VA 22310.

PORSCHE OWNERS CLUB, 6229 Outlook Ave., Los Angeles, CA 90042.

PORSCHE REGISTER, 6243 No. Oak Ave., Temple City, CA 91780.

RAILTON OWNERS CLUB, Fairmiles, Barnes Hall Rd., Burncross, Sheffield, England.

RAPIER REGISTER, 48 Ampthill Rd., Maulden, Bedfordshire, England.

REO CLUB OF AMERICA, 113 Gillin Rd., Ambler, PA 19002.

TEAM RENAULT 100 Sylvan Ave., Englewood Cliffs, NJ 07632.

REO CLUB OF CANADA, 117 Hespeler Ave., Winnipeg, Man., Canada R2L 0L5.

REO MOTORS REGISTER, Box 487, P.O. Gosford, NSW, Australia 2250.

THE RICKENBACKER CAR CLUB, RD No. 5, Box 127, Schenectady, NY 12306.

RILEY MOTOR CLUB LTD., The Gables, Hinksey Hill, Oxford, England.

RILEY REGISTER, 162 Leicester Rd., Glenhills, Leicester, England.

THE ROLLS-ROYCE OWNERS CLUB, INC., P.O. Box 25, Mechanicsburg, PA 17055.

AMICALE SALMSON, 51 Rue de Colombier, Lyon, Rhone, France.

THE SALMSON REGISTER, "Ard-na-Greina," Morley Lane, Halsemere, Surrey, England.

SIMPLEX AUTOMOBILE CLUB, Meadow Spring, Glen Cove, L.I., NY 11542.

SINGER OWNERS CLUB, 31 Rivers Hill, Watton-at-Stone, Hertford, Hertfordshire, England.

THE STANDARD REGISTER, c/o J. R. Davy, Esq., Popehill Cottage, Draycote, Rue By, CV23 9RB, England.

STAR, STARLING, STUART, & BRITON CAR REGISTER, 9 Compton Dr., Oakham, Dudley, West Midlands DY2 7ES England.

STEVENS-DURYEA ASSOCIATES, 3565 New Haven Rd., Pasadena, CA 91107.

ANTIQUE STUDEBAKER CLUB, P.O. Box 142, Monrovia, CA 91016.

STUDEBAKER DRIVERS CLUB, P.O. Box 791, Oswego, IL 60543.

STUDEBAKER OWNERS CLUB OF AMERICA, 26061 Arcada Drive, Mission Viejo, CA 92675.

AVANTI OWNERS ASSOCIATION INTERNATIONAL, Box 322, Uxbridge, MA 01569.

STUTZ NUTS, 3856 Arthington Blvd, Indianapolis, IN 46226.

SUNBEAM-TALBOT DARRACQ REGISTER, 12 Everest Road, Fishponds, Bristol, England.

AMERICAN THUNDERBIRD ASSOCIATION, Box 7484, Kansas City, MO 64116.

CLASSIC THUNDERBIRD CLUB INTERNATIONAL, Box 2398, Culver City, CA 90230.

VINTAGE THUNDERBIRD CLUB OF AMERICA, 26056 Deerfield, Dearborn Heights, MI 48127 (for squarebirds).

CLASSIC T-BIRDS, CHEVY-POWERED, c/o Robert Rosson, Box 465, Norfolk, VA 23501.

TRIUMPH CLUB OF NORTH AMERICA, 15116 Parthenia, Sepulveda, CA 91343.

TRIUMPH SPORTS OWNERS ASSOCIATION, 600 Willow Tree Rd., Leonia, NJ 07605.

VINTAGE TRIUMPH REGISTER, Box 6934, Grosse Pointe, MI 48236.

TUCKER AUTOMOBILE CLUB OF AMERICA, Box 1027, Orange Park, FL 32073.

VINCENT H.R.D. OWNERS CLUB, 132 Stockport Rd., Ashton-Under-Lyne, Lancs. England.

VOLKSWAGEN CLUB OF AMERICA, Box 963, Plainfield, NJ 07061.

UNITED KARMANN GHIA OWNERS, Box 251, LaVerne, CA 91750.

VOLVO CLUB OF NORTH AMERICA, Box 2404, Sepulveda, CA 91343.

VOLVO OWNERS UNION, Box 2234, Boulder, CO 80302.

THE WILLS CLUB, 705 So. Clyde Ave., Kissimmee, FL 32741.

WILLYS CLUB, College Arms, Apt. No. J-302, Collegeville, PA 19426.

WILLYS-OVERLAND-KNIGHT REGISTRY, 2754 Lullington Dr., Winston-Salem, NC 27103 (for vehicles through 1942).

THE WOLSELEY REGISTER, 17 Hills Ave., Cambridge CB1 4UY, England.

If you are not locked into one particular make for your first (or next) purchase, I would recommend joining the Milestone Car Society. Its focus is on 'the great cars of 1945 through 1964,' as its slogan reads. More than eighty post-WW II cars have been certified with Milestone status and they are all highly-functional automobiles.

The Milestone selection process is a democratic, meaningful procedure that has won wide-spread approval and respect throughout the old-car hobby. A member nominates a car for Milestone status by submitting the year-span, make and model, plus a brief statement attesting to its relative excellence in at least two of the following areas: design, engineering, performance, innovation or craftsmanship. These arguments are sent to a nominations committee made up of prominent experts, including people like Karl Ludvigsen, Henry Austin Clark, Jr., Lord Montagu, Michael Sedgwick, Dick Teague, Strother MacMinn and many others. This blue-ribbon panel reviews nominations and makes a recommendation by a yes or no vote on each car.

Advisors' votes and all pro and con arguments on each car are published in a newsletter with a ballot for each member. If the advisors approve a nominated car, a simple majority of members voting makes it a Milestone. If advisors disapprove, it takes a two-thirds vote of members to override them, and if more than two-thirds of the advisors disapprove, the nomination is tabled for at least six months — when it can be reconsidered if the member nominating the car in question provides additional arguments in its favor.

CERTIFIED MILESTONES: JANUARY 1976

American

BUICK RIVIERA	1949
BUICK RIVIERA	1963
BUICK SKYLARK	1953-54
CADILLAC ELDORADO BROUGHAM	1957-58
CADILLAC 60 SPECIAL	1948-49
CADILLAC 61 & 62 (CPE/CONV)	1948-49
CHEVROLET CORVETTE	1953-57
CHEVROLET CORVETTE	1963
CHEVROLET NOMAD	1955-57
CHRYSLER IMPERIAL	1951-54
CHRYSLER 300	1955-61
CHRYSLER TOWN & COUNTRY	1946-50
CONTINENTAL MARK II	1956-57
CORVAIR MONZA SPYDER	1962-64
CROSLEY HOTSHOT & SS	1950-52
CUNNINGHAM (ALL)	1951-55
DUAL GHIA	1956-58
FORD SKYLINER (RETRACTABLE)	1957-59
FORD THUNDERBIRD	1955-57
FRAZER MANHATTAN	1947-50
HUDSON	1948-54
IMPERIAL (ALL)	1955-56
JAGUAR 3.4 and 3.8	1957-64
JAGUAR XK 150	1958-61
KAISER DARRIN	1954
KAISER DELUXE/DEL. VIRGINIAN	1951-52
KAISER DRAGON	1951-53
KAISER MANHATTAN	1954-55
KAISER VAGABOND	1949-50
KAISER VIRGINIAN	1949-50
LINCOLN CAPRI	1952-54

```
LINCOLN CONTINENTAL  ..............................1946-48
LINCOLN CONTINENTAL  ..............................1961-64
OLDSMOBILE 88 (HTP/CPE/CONV)  .......................1949-50
PACKARD CARIBBEAN  ................................1953-56
PACKARD CUSTOM  ..................................1946-50
PACKARD PACIFIC & CONVERTIBLE  ...................1954
PACKARD PATRICIAN & 400  ..........................1951-56
PONTIAC SAFARI  ...................................1955-57
STUDEBAKER AVANTI  ...............................1963-64
STUDEBAKER GT HAWK  .............................1962-64
STUDEBAKER STARLIGHT COUPE  ....................1947-49
STUDEBAKER STARLIGHT COUPE  ....................1953-54
STUDEBAKER STARLINER (6 & V-8)  ..................1953-54
WILLYS-OVERLAND JEEPSTER  .......................1948-51
```

European

```
A. C. ACE & ACECA  ....................................1954-61
ALFA ROMEO GIU. SPYDER  ...........................1956-64
ALFA ROMEO GIU. SPRINT SPECIALE  ..................1959-64
ALLARD SERIES J, K2, K3  ...........................1946-56
ALUIS-3 LITRE  ......................................1954-64
ASTON MARTIN DB1 to DB4  ...........................1948-63
AUSTIN HEALEY 100 & 100M  .........................1953-56
BENTLEY (ALL)  ....................................1946-64
BMW 507  ..........................................1957-59
CISITALIA GT BY PININFARINA  .......................1946-49
CITROEN DS19 & ID19  ..............................1955-64
DELAGE D.6  .......................................1946-49
DELAHAYE 135, 175 & 180  ..........................1946-51
FACEL VEGA (ALL V-8'S)  ............................1954-64
FERRARI (ALL V-12'S)  ..............................1947-64
HEALEY SILVERSTONE  ..............................1949-50
JAGUAR XK120-XK150  ..............................1948-54
JAGUAR E-TYPE  ...................................1961-64
LANCIA FLAMINIA ZAGOTA  ..........................1959-64
LOTUS ELITE  ......................................1958-63
M.G. "TC"  ........................................1946-49
MASERATI 3500 GT  .................................1957-64
MERCEDES-BENZ 220SE (CPE/CONV)  ..................1957-64
MERCEDES-BENZ 300 (ALL TYPES)  ...................1952-64
MERCEDES-BENZ 600  ...............................1964
MORGAN PLUS FOUR  ...............................1950-64
NASH-HEALEY  .....................................1951-54
NSU WANKEL SPYDER  ..............................1964
PEGASO  ..........................................1951-58
PORSCHE SERIES 356  ..............................1949-64
RILEY 2.5 RMA-RME  ...............................1945-55
ROLLS-ROYCE (ALL)  ...............................1947-64
TALBOT LAGO 4.5 & RECORD  ........................1946-54
TRIUMPH TR2 & TR3  ...............................1953-63
TRIUMPH ROADSTER 1800-2000  .....................1946-50
```

Specials & Low Production

BUGATTI TYPE 101 1951
LAGONDA V-12 1948-49
PACKARD PANTHER DAYTONA 1954
TUCKER '48 1948
WOODILL WILDFIRE 1952-58

For further information on The Milestone Car Society write to: M.C.S., Box 1166Z, Pacific Palisades, California, 90272.

Club members can be especially valuable in suggesting and locating alternatives to models you may be contemplating. Yet you should never stop listening to that little voice inside you that says: "This design I like, and that design I don't (including interior layout and seating comfort at the steering wheel).

Major cities in all states tend to have many helpful club members. Learn who they are through the national office of the club(s) in which you have an interest, and visit the people. You will learn firsthand (without buying) if that car in your memories still quickens your heartbeat.

10 Establishing Current Values

There are several important interplaying factors that determine a car's value:

    (1) condition

    (2) public acceptance of the particular make and model

    (3) acceptance the car receives from automotive experts and collectors (different than factor number 2)

    (4) scarcity, based largely on original production numbers

    (5) performance, durability and availability of parts and service

    (6) its position on the Depreciation/ Reappreciation Chart (Chapter 2)

    (7) your personal likes and dislikes

Your own likes are last on this list, but are given headline billing in Chapter 6. Obviously, they should strongly influence all your selections. Much more fun that way! Never-forget the other factors, though, if you are out to recoup your investment as well.

The owner of a 1971 Cadillac, upon learning that I was writing this book, asked if he could simply keep his current car for twenty-five years, and make a good investment. All seven factors come into play in answering. First, to live with a car that long, it has to be a car that he likes and that treats him well. And he is more apt to keep it up to snuff if he knows he owns a well-engineered, attractive car to start with. Parts and service availability are not substantially different from one make to another. The result is that the cars which do get top-flight service, especially the exotic models, reappreciate sooner. Folks who pick exotic cars and underestimate repairs end up with a tiger's tail, and dubious appreciation potential.

It is possible to combine all these factors and maximize your potential. I did this on a 1956 Mercedes-Benz 300Sc roadster, which I owned for more than ten years. I drove it 100,000 miles, and it sold for nearly fifty percent more than I paid for it. This particular model Mercedes-Benz is highly-respected by nearly everyone in the motorcar world (factors 2 and 3), and it was certified a Milestone car by ninety-two percent of the voting membership. Plus, this was a fuel-injected model of which only fifty-three roadsters were ever built (factor 4), and until recently there existed an above-average network of factory-trained dealers and factory parts availability (factor 5).

Stir these factors together gently and a supercar emerges with potential so great it is hard to do anything that will threaten its growth to staggering five-figure values over the long term.

Maintenance on these supercars is expensive, as we have already discussed. Qualified repairmen sometimes charge more than $20 per hour. All totaled though, including insurance and over $5,000 in maintenance costs on my Mercedes-Benz, the cost of ownership at 100,000 miles was less than eight cents per mile! Had I babied the car, held the mileage down and correspondingly kept maintenance bills and wear-and-tear down, the investment would have rivaled the best in the world. Maybe it did anyway. Had I sold the car five

MERCEDES-BENZ 300Sc: This 1970 photo shows the author (right) and Robert Wittenberg of Milwaukee, Wisconsin, receiving tie first-place awards in class at the Mercedes-Benz Club of America's National Meet at Elkhart Lake, Wisconsin. Only 200 of these hand-built, fuel-injected personal cars were built. They had two enormous, reclining bucket front seats in full leather and a small, combination jump-seat and luggage rack in the rear. Three versions — coupe, roadster and cabriolet — were available from 1955 to 1958. Engine, transmission and differential-axle design were nearly identical to the 300SL. To my way of thinking, this model captures more of the old Mercedes-Benz tradition and appearance, yet also has more of the very modern Mercedes-Benz attributes than any other single Mercedes in the firm's eighty-year history. Wheelbase: 114.7 inches. Its 183-cubic inch engine delivered 200 horsepower. The fuel injection system was a Bosch direct-block system, the first offered as standard equipment in any passenger car in the world — and remarkably trouble-free in operation.

years later, other things being equal, my sale price would have jumped fifty percent more.

It will be a rare car that meets all the conditions listed at the beginning of this chapter. Some exotic cars, like the Facel Vega, while held in high esteem by knowledgeable collectors (factor no. 3) are so little known by the general public (factor no. 2) that resale comes

1954-63 MERCEDES-BENZ 300SL: The 'gull-wing' coupe was in a class by itself. The original selling price was an unbelievably low $7,200; twenty years later an authentically preserved or restored example commands three or more times that amount. Beware of restoration costs if you see one for sale; engine rebuilding alone will exceed $2,500 — plus transmission, fuel injection, body work, paint and interior. There are no bargains in this marque; everyone knows exactly what they've got. Unless you inherit one, you will have to pay the price! My 300Sc had the basic 183-cubic inch (three-liter) engine, 'detuned' to 200 horsepower from 240, and I can report incredibly durable performance of all components. At 100,000 miles the brake shoes (four inches wide) were only two-thirds worn. On the other hand, the factory price for a regulator was $56; a Chevrolet Corvette regulator was, at the most, $7 at that time. The roadster version of the 300SL is nearly as desirable as the 'gull-wing.' It had a number of mechanical improvements, and was easier to enter and exit. It was built until 1963. Both 300SL's brought a new level of refinement to sports cars.

slowly. This does not affect their proper value but it does appreciably affect liquidity — the speed of converting the asset into cash. This need not concern the well-heeled purchaser who won't *have* to sell. There are buyers for these 'kings' chariots,' but not every little hamlet has that sophisticated a king.

Conversely, most Fords will never be Milestones (factor no. 3); but there are many past Ford owners ready to get nostalgic about acquiring your well-preserved old Ford (factor 2). If liquidity is important to you, I suggest sticking closely to popular, high-volume manufacturers that are still in business.

Since personal preference, age and the car's condition are all factors, it is not possible to say that any one model will always draw the highest price, though some come close; e.g., the Tucker or the Mercedes-Benz 300SL.

Car investment can be treated much more like house investment than is commonly recognized. Proper house repairs, a well-manicured neighborhood, architectural design — all add to your score card when sale time comes along. The same is true for automobiles. Choose a significant design, with top-of-the-line equipment, even if you were not motivated to do so in past car purchases.

11 Buying the Car: Private Sources vs. Auctions

Once you have settled on a model or two that you like, becoming familiar with current prices is the next task. Study the magazine advertisements. For $15 to $25 in phone calls to owners and dealers around the country, you will become an expert on the current price range and condition of cars of any specific year and make (perhaps more knowledgeable than most of the sellers). I favor the phone; letters are so time-consuming that many sellers won't even reply, especially if they are getting enough phone inquiries. You can request photos of the car if you like what sellers say on the phone; but I've learned that even that is of marginal value, since most photos (color or black and white) are either too handsome (don't reveal even the true condition of the paint), or are so poorly taken that they turn you off to what may be a good automobile.

If you know what the particular model basically looks like, visualize it in your mind, and ask very specific questions about its various components. A typical conversation might go like this:

YOU: "Mr. McKenzie, I'm calling about the 1959 Ford Retractable Hardtop you have advertised. I'm calling long distance from (your town)."

Always mention where you are calling from if you have dialed direct, as you will generally get more candor if the seller knows you are far away. He knows you would be pretty miffed to travel 500 miles to buy his car only to learn it was misrepresented.

McKENZIE: "Why yes, of course. What can I tell you?"

If you have access to a WATS line, you may want to

1957 FORD FAIRLANE 500 SKYLINER: Ford built 48,394 of these machines between 1957-59. Fewer than two hundred remain on the road. Chrysler, GM and several European firms built a handful of retractable solid roofs (mostly show cars). The top is operated by seven motors, ten relays, ten limit-switches and 610 feet of wire. It was designed to withstand 10,000 closing-opening cycles without failure. Ninteen fifty-seven was the first year of this basic body style for all Fords; some enthusiasts regard the design of the 1957 Fairlane 500 series as having the most appealing lines of any post-1945 Ford. Not short, body length jumped nine inches in 1957 to a total of 208 inches. Wheelbase: 118 inches. In 1957, optional power included a 312-cubic inch V-8 generating 145 hp.

leave the initial conversation open-ended and see how the seller describes his car first. Listen for the finesse of his description, and if he makes statements like "good for a 1959 car" or "I'm not a collector so I don't know" — beware. The healthiest signs are straight-shooting answers: "Well sir, there are pits in the chrome on the rear bumper and tail light rings, but the rest of the trim and front bumper are outstanding." Without a WATS line, after perhaps a minute of listening to him, you'll want to get down to a specific checklist of items you have prepared in advance. Ask the same questions on all calls so that you have a standard for comparison. It also gives you a feel for how different sellers respond to the same questions . . . confidently, with qualifications, defensively.

YOU: "Do you know the history of the car's previous owners?"

McKENZIE: "Yes, I bought it from a man in Silver Springs. He gave me all his service records. He rebuilt the engine and repainted the car in 1970."

YOU: "Was he the original owner?"

McKENZIE: "No, I think he got it from his uncle or some other relative."

History can be revealing. We have already discussed repainting, which becomes difficult to assess. A sale shortly after engine rebuilding! Why?

YOU: "How many actual miles are on the car, do you know?"

McKENZIE: "Speedometer reads 62,000. Interior is in good condition, so I assume the mileage is correct."

That's not solid enough. "The speedometer says" is a scapegoat. What does he say? No assumptions al-

lowed in this department! Either the mileage is confirmed or it is meaningless. McKenzie said he got a lot of past service records. Hmmm.

YOU: "Mr. McKenzie, you mentioned getting many service records. Have you checked them to see if there is any logical sequence of mileage with the current odometer reading?"

McKENZIE: "No. I'll be glad to check it for you."

YOU: "Yes, please do that. If I purchase the car I would also want the name of the prior owner and service papers. Is that possible?"

McKENZIE: "Yes."

I always ask for a specific comment on each of the following:

YOU: "How is the glass? Any of it chipped or cracked?"

McKENZIE: "It's all good. There might be a small stone chip or two on the windshield, but they are very small. None of the glass has fogged from age."

YOU: "Is it tinted glass?"

McKENZIE: "I don't think so."

YOU: "How about the upholstery? Is it leather or vinyl?"

McKENZIE: "It's vinyl. It's in pretty good shape. It's a little faded, but no rips. There is some stitching loose by the driver's seat."

YOU: "How about the carpeting?"

McKENZIE: "It's original and very good except the driver's area."

YOU: "How about the body? Any rust points?"

McKENZIE: "The car originally came from Kansas and has not been exposed to much salt. There's no visible rust anywhere on the paint. The rocker panels look good."

Based on these remarks, it is very likely the car has at least 62,000 miles. The worn carpeting and seats are some evidence of this and you can plan on at least a few hundred dollars for wear-and-tear-type restoration even if the motor is excellent.

It is usually worth the added price to buy a car that has not been exposed to salt streets and salt air. Rusty fenders and rocker panels (under doors) can be properly repaired if caught soon enough. Rust's nickname, 'body cancer,' is quite apropos; happily, it is not always terminal. Nevertheless, it costs as much or more to repair a rusty car as it does to buy a car that has never seen rust.

YOU: "Please give me as much information on the engine as possible. What components are you sure have been replaced?"

McKENZIE: "The motor was completely rebuilt by the previous owner three years ago."

YOU: "Do you know how many miles it has been driven since the overhaul?"

McKENZIE: "I'd guess 15,000 miles."

YOU: "Do you know if the battery, generator/alternator, transmission or cooling system have had work?"

McKENZIE: "Yes. As a matter of fact, I've done nearly all of these items myself in the past eighteen months. Flushed the radiator and put a new water pump on, too."

"I've spent about $150 on front suspension work and the car has two new shock absorbers."

YOU: "How does the car's retractable top work?"

McKENZIE: "No problems — runs good. No leaks."

It's possible our Mr. McKenzie is offering a car for sale because of his recent rash of repairs. If he isn't very patient, he may be ready to give up a car that is actually very desirable, especially with the work that he has done on it.

Shortly after college I had an opportunity to buy a six-year-old car that appeared to be quite nice on the dealer's lot. I asked permission to talk to the prior owner, who confessed that starting the cold engine had always worried him as it turned over too slowly. I bought the car and added a 124-amp tractor battery. It was a shame the prior owner didn't do that . . . he gave up a mighty fine car.

Phone inquiries, of course, are not the same as seeing and driving the car, but I have done just enough chasing around the country to appreciate how much important screening can be done by phone. Also, comparing prices with a few phone calls could save you hundreds of dollars on the car you do buy. You come to your final purchase point on an equal or better footing with the seller if there is any negotiating to be done. You will also learn of parts sources that might not be volunteered in written communication.

Here is an idea that I have used successfully when one or two cars which sound reasonable by phone are located out of town or out of state (which is entirely probable if you are using national advertising sources). If you have joined one or more of those clubs listed in the previous chapter, check their membership rosters. See if one of the members lives near your prospective car's location. It doesn't have to be someone saving the same make you are considering, either, though the same general vintage is desirable. Milestone Car Society (MCS) members would be good for 1945 to late sixties' cars. Classic Car Club members would be of assistance on pre-WW II cars. Give one of them a call; explain that you are hundreds of miles away. Based on his apparent knowledge of and interest in cars, would he be kind enough to look at it, and call you collect with his opinion? Chances are he will be flattered to be asked. He will probably also consider it an insult if you offer to pay him; however, good manners insist that you cover his costs: about fifteen cents a mile. You will rarely find someone within fifteen miles of the car, which amounts to about $10.00 *minimum* out-of-pocket cost for him. But if he really helps you, sending him $10-20 sure beats a long trip by you as the second step in your quest.

This third-party opinion, while provided by someone you have never met, can confirm your concerns or enthusiasms about the car in question before you take to the air (or road) to see it yourself. I once had such a good report from a fellow MCS member that I bought a car sight unseen, and had it shipped to me. Nervous about my boldness, I rushed to the truck on delivery day, and found the most handsome, pristine car I have ever owned. I still own it.

One of the more conspicuous oc-curences in the car hobby is the auction. Auctions have caused much discussion and strong feelings within the hobby. Their publicity boasts of an investment arena unrivaled any-where. National promotions and news reports of their results have narrowed regional dif-ferences in car values. The true rarity of cer-tain cars has become more evident as the pressures of supply and demand interact. Col-lectors themselves have mixed emotions about these developments. They see car and parts prices climbing from 25¢ to $2 on the dollar. Owners see their hobby costs climbing. "Damn commercialism!" they shout. "Outlaw the auc-tions!" "Ban their ads." "They're ruining the hobby."

I'm certain the aggressive activity of sev-eral international auction firms has greatly influenced car values. There are other consid-erations, however.

The search for quality cars of any vin-tage can be very trying and costly. For exam-ple, I recently have been looking for a collecti-ble car for personal use that I'll drive about 5,000 miles per year. I want something with a relatively short wheelbase that's easy to handle, easy on gas; possibly a convertible — and in A-1 condition.

A few recognized Milestones that fit this description are the Porsche 356, Austin Healey 100-4, Triumph TR 2/3, Nash-Healey, Kaiser-

Darrin, the six-cylinder Corvettes and small-engined 1955-57 Thunderbirds. After spending several weekends and more miles than I can believe, I'd only seen eight cars and none of them was really what I wanted. A certain amount of this is fun, and it tests one's good judgment, but the cost of one's time eventually overrides the pleasure. Eighty percent of all cars advertised are not worth buying, which may not surprise you. The trick is to find ways of cutting through that eighty percent as swiftly as possible.

The typical 'old car' auction brings together 100 to 250 cars in one location at one time. For an entry fee of $2 to $4, you can look over more 'for sale' collector cars than you could see in six months of weekends. Some will be bummers, and some will be fit for a maharaja. Much fanfare will surround the very expensive merchandise, but whatever your specific price range, you'll probably find much to compare at a good car auction, with all cars conveniently parked side-by-side.

Drop by the night before, and owners will start the engines and even let you drive around (within the auction compound) to 'feel' the merchandise. You won't have a hoist, so I recommend that, before the bidding begins, you crawl under each car of interest — with a flashlight — to compare undercarriages. Superficial restorations look good beneath the floodlights, but come unglued in a matter of months. One of the reasons car auctions are held inside tents or buildings is that cars look better under artificial lights. You can be caught

Auction Sales of old cars in the United States totaled over $50 million during 1975. Here
one of the most well-known firms, the Kruse Auction Company, hawks a classic roadster
to a typical crowd. Bud Josey (lower right in white shirt), proprietor of the Horseless
Carriage Shop in Dunedin, Florida, and James Southard, president of Classic Car In-

estments in Atlanta, Georgia, watch Dean Kruse, auctioneer. This writer's experience is
that eighty percent of the cars that sell at auctions are bid close to their true value. One
car in ten is a bargain; one in ten sells at too high a price.

off guard if something interesting arrives on the auction block that you haven't examined beforehand.

Even if your objectives are seventy-five percent to place investment dollars, I'd urge you to consider only cars you've a planned rationale for buying. If you find such cars have been entered, sign up for your bidder's number (usually $10) and get ready for the auction.

Since the publication of the first edition of this book, I have served as Car Advisor to a number of old-car auctions. I can report that they have no more mystique than your mind brings to them. The question of auction ethics arises occasionally. The basic auction format hasn't changed for centuries. If the auctioneer can slip in a non-existent bidder now and then, that's considered his risk as much as the bidder's. He knows the danger of being stuck with that bid and having to backtrack to a lower bid too many times for the same audience. If shills (phony bidders) are planted in the crowd, they risk getting stuck as the highest bidder on a car they are trying to help sell, not buy. Outlawing these tactics never solves the problem; doing so would be as ineffective as Prohibition was. Controlling shills would be impossible — who would do it? Besides, most frequent offenders are car owners, not the auctioneer. The auctioneer's antics are integral to the process. It's his job to draw out the top dollar from the bidders.

One practice useful in auctioning 'big ticket' items such as cars is the seller's right to set a minimum price below which he will not sell. No secret bids are required, and all bidders know a minimum exists. Some debate has occurred about announcing each minimum price before bidding commences. This has been tried, largely unsuccessfully. It markedly restricts initial bidding — which auctioneers say is necessary to loosen up the key bidders on each offering. It is nearly universal practice to announce the owner's minimum if bidding doesn't reach his price; occasionally an owner will lower his minimum *during* bidding. The auctioneer will announce this to all when it occurs.

You can usually learn the owner's minimum price before the auction, but don't let that mislead you, as owners sometimes know no more about correct pricing than you do. You may know more! His motivations naturally include getting as high a price as he can. You would want to, too. But depending on the distance he's traveled, and his reasons for offering to sell, he may change his price before going home. This is another edge to the process to keep in mind. If bids *from others* are nowhere near the seller's minimum, you stand a reasonable chance the owner's minimum will soften immediately after the auction. There is some risk in this. I have occasionally seen a surprise sale — an owner suddenly removed his minimum, even when the top bid was thousands of dollars lower. The auctioneer shouted "Sold" to an astonished crowd when everyone expected the offer to be refused. The point is, don't stay totally out of the bidding.

Don't feed it too quickly, either. Two watch-words here: (1) More bidding time is allowed on vehicles that exceed $3,000–$5,000; there's more at stake for everyone. (2) Don't forget to locate your competitive bidders as they bid, to be sure they exist, and watch their convictions, hesitation, etc.

If you bring a car to sell at an auction, one consideration is positioning the car in the line-up. Is it best to be placed early, midday, or late? Officially, sequence is decided by the auction company, but you can usually influence it if you feel strongly enough. Except, maybe, for avoiding the first and last twenty-five cars, I have little preference. Most auctions drag out to become a long day; starting at 10 a.m. and going beyond 6 p.m. With a car every three minutes — that's twenty per hour. It's impossible to predict the bidders' collective habits, their lunch times or other interruptions. People do key into particular cars or types of cars. To say that your car will bring a higher price if it comes up to the block just before lunch rather than between 2 and 3 p.m., is impossible. The true condition of the car on auction day is far more important. Despite the many novices coming into the hobby annually, I have to marvel at the general accuracy with which bidders treat a car's merits. Quality merchandise draws top prices. Mediocre cars bring mediocre bids. Average cars draw average prices. In my experience, approximately one car in every ten is bought at an unreasonably high price, and one in ten is 'stolen' for well below market value. Everyone likes to believe he made the buy of the hour. As a generalization, I'd have to say the majority get what they paid for. Those who overpay have time on their side, if they don't underestimate restoration costs.

A company in Portland, Oregon — Auto Futurity, Inc. — has applied a computer process developed by Rand Corporation to identify the effect time will have on car values. Called the Delphi Technique, it makes systematic use of expert opinion. Specific cars are presented to a group, with detailed specifications, and the question: "In your estimation, in what year will the above automobile of average condition (used but cared for) become worth twice today's price?" Their forecasts are computed and refined four times to arrive at a concensus. In *all* results I have seen vehicles double in value in less than eight years, with some as soon as four years. Auto Futurity's 1975 results for the 1967 Ferrari 330 GTC project a value of $15,000 in 1983. With an original list price of $14,700, this value places it exactly on the upper curve of my Reappreciation Chart in Chapter 2, recovering its original list price eighteen years after it was built. A rare-bodied Ferrari would outperform this achievement.

The prediction for the original series 1963 Avanti is among the highest of all time. Its 1975 value is expected to double by 1979. It has already recovered its original list price in the past ten to twelve years. I believe this is without precedent in American cars. Certain recent German cars in the U.S. have exceeded their original list price on the used car market due solely to the severe shift in exchange rates between Deutsche marks and dollars. This phenomenon is not at work on the Avanti, which makes the Avanti's rise in value all the more phenomenal.

12 Inspecting the Car

After scouting about, and assuming you do not buy over the phone, you are ready to make your first on-site car inspection. Since eighty percent of all cars advertised are not worth buying there is more value in improving your odds by phone. Even with many phone calls, fifty percent may prove to be unacceptable merchandise. Yet the prizes of earnest searching will be worth every minute!

Paint finish will be the most misleading. A shiny finish may fool your senses as much as a dull finish. Neither is especially predictive of the rest of the car. If you like its outside appearance you should, if possible, put the car on a hoist at a local gas station or garage. Make a checklist so that you can preserve your objectivity as much as possible. After all, you may have travelled many miles — so your ego has a stake in the travel investment you have already made. It's very painful to walk away from a prospective car when you get this close — even if the car doesn't come up to the image you have formed before arrival.

Assume that *any* repairs needed will cost twice as much as the first figure that pops into your mind. Dollars, plus your time! Here I repeat my conviction that people are ahead of the game to pay more for an original, clearly well-maintained or professionally restored car than to buy deteriorated, unrestored merchandise. You *will*, with iron patience, locate good merchandise. Even if you seek an exotic model, there is usually someone saving one for you somewhere. Second, as a beginning participant in this field, don't take on more work than you really have to. A thorough maintenance and moderate upgrading plan is all you should attempt with your first purchase. Later, if you begin to enjoy a car for its own sake — well, maybe then get into restoration.

Onward to our inspection checklist. You have my permission to duplicate it to your heart's content. Correspondingly, your suggestions for improvements are sought for future printings of this book. You can partially fill out one of these forms during phone conversations to help you recall details you might otherwise forget. Mark them as phone notes, or on-site notes, so that six weeks later you won't forget which are which.

Many a shock is produced by a car's underside. Be prepared to see the usual collection of grease and surface rust (e.g., on the muffler). Most owners never think about their undercarriages until they hear a bad muffler, or see a hole in their floorboard or fender. Shiny body paint, you bet, but it's a godsend to find someone who maintains his car's undercarriage beyond the chassis lubrication points. In many cars what you see will be quite fixable, unless salt has eaten away large pieces. Most cars need some muffler work. Check and smell the transmission fluid for burnt or pungent odor. Do universal joints have slack? Depending on the car you are looking at, universals will be nearly anywhere these days in swinging independent rear axles, at the drive shaft, and of course near the front wheels and front transmission on the Toronado and some Eldorados.

Serious problems will make audible sounds as you drive down the road; listen carefully. Sounds are very revealing.

(1) A dash *buzz* is often in the speedometer cable.

(2) A mild *howl* or *growl* when the engine is running could be in the transmission, bearings, clutch or drive shaft.

(3) An engine *knock* may be in main bearings, connecting rods or piston pins.

(4) A *hum* at the rear when a car is gaining speed is usually a rear axle problem.

(5) A *hiss* around the engine could be caused by air escaping from a vacuum hose, a loose spark plug or a faulty heat-riser tube.

(6) *Rattles* are usually caused by metal hitting metal — a muffler hitting the frame, a loose bolt on a shock absorber, a fan blade or a window lift mechanism.

EXAMINATION
Of Condition and Repair Costs

The purpose of this form is two-fold: First, to spot weaknesses in the car at this point in time, and then to evaluate your cost to correct. Don't underprice your own time.

Car Make _____ Model _____ Date _____

Color _____ Special Features _____ Year _____

Owner _____ Address _____

City _____ Phones: Home _____ Work _____

	Out-standing	Good	Pass-able	Needs Work	Needs Change	Cost or Hours to correct

BODY CONDITION
1. Paint, if original, can it be saved. If repaint, check quality of surface and overspray.
2. Chrome — consider size of bad pieces.
3. Glass — consider especially rare or curved pieces.
4. Top(s), fender skirts, emblems and accessories.
5. Body damage and general cleanliness.

UNDERCARRIAGE
1. Cleanliness, absence of extra grease. Locate sources of oil and grease leaks.
2. Rusted or bare metal needing repair; esp. check wheel wells, rocker and fender panels.
3. Muffler system and shock absorbers.
4. Tires, evenness of tire wear (alignment).

ENGINE AND TRUNK COMPARTMENT

1. History and miles since major overhaul, and age of starter, water pump, battery, etc.
2. Scratches and cleanliness on metal surfaces, i.e., frequent or careless repairs.
3. Electrical wiring safety and neatness. Age of radiator, hoses and belts.
4. Trunk cleanliness, condition of mat, spare, jack and tools.

INTERIOR

1. Door panels, hardware, door seals.
2. Original seats, armrests, carpets.
3. Dash, dials, buttons, pedals, steering wheel.
4. Operation of wipers, horn, brake lights, direction lights, hand brake, radio, heater, air conditioner (not just fans), all power equipment.

GENERAL DRIVING

1. Engine idle and muffler noises or smoke.
2. Handling, body and engine sounds: check on bumpy road and on highway 10 mph faster than you normally would drive the car.
3. General preservation and appearance.

TOTAL NUMBER CHECKS & COSTS

Conclusion: Near perfect restorations and originals **are** available. Double your estimate of correction costs (unless you are very sure they are sound) and add to asking price. This is your true cost if driving and reappreciation are sought. Weigh this price against the alternative vehicles you are considering.

(7) *Squeals* are typically caused by a slipping or old fan belt, worn or unlubricated water pump or bad brushes in the generator. Brakes and tires can also squeal.

(8) A *snappity-snap* from the engine may be caused by a cracked distributor cap, broken or bare spark plug wires, or loose connections.

Listen cautiously for clues. To identify what's going on is not to declare a car a basket case, but rather is an attempt to accurately assess a car's costs beyond the purchase price. Learn to be quite sensitive to the slightest irregular sounds. Some will be inherent characteristics. And some will belong to another car running nearby, as I occasionally discover to my embarrassment. Hearing irregular, small sounds before they shout can save you hundreds of dollars by repairing early or avoiding purchase. When a noise or other item bothers you, get a specific report from the seller on it. There may be an easy solution. Then, too, discussing these weaknesses strengthens your negotiating position.

13 Preparing Your Own Maintenance Plan

In this book's title I say "And enjoy every minute." I do. And you can, but whether with a new car or collectible used car, I'll admit the second pleasure sometimes comes from success in detecting good or bad service before the fact (first is the excitement of purchase). It is a crime against humanity to be human at times; the simple truth is that service managers, mechanics and parts men frequently have other priorities (commission incentives and flat rates) different from those of the owner. Add to this the sad and amusing problems of simple communication, and you're off to the unfortunate but standard start. Few consumer action groups are demanding excellence or legislated standards for automobile repair shops.[12] There are many obvious conflicts of interest between businessman and customer, from piecework pay incentives to full component replacement. Practices that serve the businessman's objectives will serve the customer's objectives only some of the time.

The public's weak stand on these matters over the years has netted them what they deserve: the 'disposable' car, as this book's photo of a rusted two-year old Chevrolet Vega shows. That is exactly what some of the 'economy' cars of the seventies offer right off the assembly line.

The first step to satisfaction is to be aware of the prevailing orientation among the majority of service departments and repairmen, and to make your differing objectives known to a person in the business who will listen more than superficially.

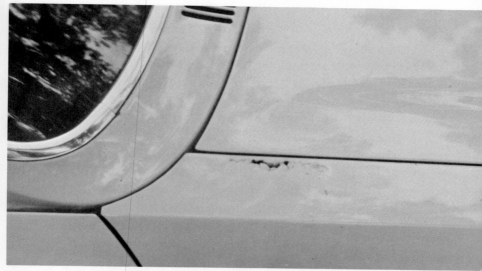

DISPOSABLE CARS: Antithesis to a car preserved as a permanent asset, this Chevrolet Vega celebrated its second anniversary the month this photo was taken. At twenty-four months, it was rusted completely through from the inside out! After more than three decades of automobile rust problems, you'd think Detroit could lick the problem. But car manufacturers or their dealers seldom show any interest; so our routine inspections, rust-proof paint and oil coatings must end the nuisance. People take better care of their $500 fishing boats than they do their $5,000 motorcars. It is common sense that constant exposure to the weather demands annual preventive maintenance. Don't wait for your local car dealer to suggest it. You must take the initiative.

In many cities shops specialize in servicing older cars; you will also be pleasantly rewarded to discover the friendly subculture of folks with objectives similar to your own.

My preference is to buy only well-restored or original cars, and to direct my activity to keeping them in top shape. Even if you are sure that restoration is your bag, rather than frequent driving, I still cannot recommend very much restoration — especially if this is your first or second venture. If too much work is necessary, the rewards of driving may be destroyed.

One should learn many things about any car, new or used. Since your new pride and joy is going to become a more personal member of the family than would the 'disposable' car, you will want to follow a maintenance plan very conscientiously. It will be the maintenance that separates the lesser cars from the high prices some cars command five and ten years into the future.

Several new books advertised in the hobby magazines concentrate on restoring cars, so I will assume this step is covered and concentrate on maintenance and a moderate program of regular, permanent improvements. I would also recommend adding a book entitled *How to Get Your Car Repaired Without Getting Gypped*[13] to your library. It describes numerous traps in the car repair industry and suggests specialized solutions. Of course, the ultimate answer is an ethical mechanic who puts modern diagnosis first and has no conflicting pay incentives.

Driving your car is essential. Running the engine at 2500-3500 rpm regularly is also necessary for good lubrication and engine firing. Some cars, especially ones with precision-built engines (such as Mercedes-Benz), actually thrive on brisk engine use. Parts stay better lubricated, and thus more responsive to your call — just as physical fitness is commensurate with exercising. For this reason, the finest historic automobiles are generally driven by their museum staff on a routine basis. The charts in Part I assume 10,000 miles per year. In actual practice, since many people have several cars, 5,000 miles is as likely an average, and the actual replacement of components will be proportionally less frequent than the example in Chapter 2.

Schedule routine work like oil changes, chassis lubrications, brake inspections, etc., by the calendar, regardless of mileage per year, unless you use synthetic oil, which I recommend for selected use in post-1945 cars. Work can be done by your local gas station if you know the owner, and if he and his mechanic respect the thorough care you seek. To some extent, the distinctive car you drive will help convey the message 'handle with care.' Oil filters sometimes cost twice as much at service stations and new car dealerships than at your local discount centers, but depending on the value of your own time it can be worth this cost to save chasing across town for parts and installing them. The air filter is another story. You can replace it yourself as easily as a home air conditioning filter, without getting messy.

The pre-1960 cars frequently have an oil bath air cleaner that doesn't require filter replacement. Ask your serviceman to change that oil once a year. (More often in dusty areas, per the owner's manual).

So much for the easy stuff. Many of you, especially those of you who live where there is salt, are justly concerned about rust. Obviously, you will try to avoid rust when buying a car in the first place. The cost of refinishing a rusty car is usually equal to the price difference for rust-free cars when your own time for repairs is counted. Even if you have rust-free cars, driving them and keeping them rust-free requires some strategy. The traditional American method of undercoating cars with a tar-like covering (such as Ziebart) is good, if expertly applied. The usual problem is that corners get missed, or trapped dirt or moisture (even on new cars) prevent the compound from thoroughly sticking. Once moisture gets behind the undercoating, the result is just as bad as salt. Unless I am (1) very positive of a car's dryness and cleanliness and (2) able to discuss specific peculiarities of the undercarriage with the man doing the job, and (3) driving in winter or frequently-changing temperatures . . . I would not undercoat my car's undercarriage.

Instead, I would clean it well — steam clean it if necessary — and:
- (1) use a rust dissolver where necessary
- (2) pull all loose undercoating off
- (3) repaint all metal surfaces (avoiding rubber hoses and rubber) with two

coats of anti-rust paint

(4) if the car will be in concours displays, a third coat in a conservative, complementary color is also in order

(5) spray the entire undercarriage (except the exhaust system) with an oil preservative twice a year

(6) paint the exhaust system with 1200-degree paint (stainless steel tail pipes, as expensive as they are, will prove more economical in the long run)

(7) perform an annual inspection and touch-up

This all sounds like a pain, but the cost of hiring someone to do it probably will not exceed the cost of a conventional Ziebart-quality undercoating job. On a car that has been used for more than a few months it is too late to use regular undercoating without the above steps anyway. But think what you will have accomplished! You will have taken strong precautions against the most undermining and insidious of all car problems. It will have been well worth it, and much less expensive than cutting rusty metal off and replacing it later. Cutting and replacing, incidentally, is what you must do if you have rust. Face up to it, plastic has its place in body repairs, but it rarely solves a rust problem; it only hides it. You will fool very few people and be haunted yourself if rust is still working behind there. Besides, a plastic job costs two-thirds of doing a proper metal replacement job.

Even the largest manufacturers could

care less about rust problems. It used to take more than five years for a car's fenders to rust through, even with hard use. Perhaps this is another area (like pollution safety and gas mileage standards), where the public must make Detroit take serious notice of a problem (i.e., pressure for more stringent standards). I have little sympathy for Detroit, on the one hand; they have known about the rapid effects of salt and moisture on cars for decades. The public's weak response, on the other hand, has encouraged mass-production-oriented Detroit to opt for the disposable automobile. Body changes, we may conclude, seldom reduce rust weaknesses.

Styling seldom improves with body change either. Some of the most brilliant post-war designs are more than twenty years old: 1953 Studebaker by Raymond Loewy,[14] 1956 Continental Mark II, 1948 Cisitalia now in the permanent collection of the Museum of Modern Art, New York City, to name only three. We joke about a few odd folks in New York City setting men's and women's fashions for the whole nation. I sometimes suspect that the same thing has happened at our automotive design studios.

In post-WW II cars, two areas that reflect rapidly increasing styling sophistication and maintenance requirements are bodies and electrical systems. The drive-train components haven't changed that much even through the sixties. The successful post-1950 collector must, at an early stage, come to amicable terms with the eccentricities of his car's body and electronics. If he doesn't, it is doubtful that he will be a happy owner.

Our cars house more accessories than ever before, and generally contain more compartments, corners, panels, insulation, screws, fasteners and wires. The past twenty-five years has brought us the blooming of technology, from signal-seeking radios with electric antennas to power steering and air-conditioning. Before the war, and afterwards for many car builders, there lingered a feeling of "Let's avoid complicated devices." Rolls-Royce and Mercedes-Benz were very slow to standardize electric windows and automatic transmissions.

CONTINENTAL MARK II: Slightly more than 3,000 of these largely hand-built cars were produced during 1956 and 1957. Hand-picked, specially-prepared Lincoln engines were used: A V-8 of 368 cubic inches (six liters) developed approximately 285-300 horsepower. Four hundred to 415 ft-lb of torque sped the 4,825-pound chariot to 120 mph in impressive silence. Ford Motor Company has been a long-standing leader in efforts to cut annoying engine and wind noises and general road vibrations, though they did not take the lead in air suspension. A brief, unsuccessful offering of Ford-Aire and Mercury Air Cushion Ride in 1958 luckily did not appear on the Mark II. Handling was typically American — great on the expressway, though a tad (or two tads) heavy for outstanding cornering or close-in maneuverability. Rust is a slight problem; inspect repainted bodies closely to learn what may be hidden. If restoration bills are available for inspection, the caliber of the work can sometimes be evaluated. Wheelbase: 126 inches.

While air-conditioning was first offered in production models by Packard in 1938, Cadillac and Lincoln did not feature it in their sales literature until 1953 and 1956 respectively (both, however, offered it earlier upon request). Quite suddenly, between 1952 and 1957, a revolution of electronic devices broke the code of simplicity, and thousands of gismos were available from every manufacturer. Don't curse these accessories or remove any of them when they fail to work. Non-functional accessories have driven some collectors to stay with the simpler cars of the twenties and thirties. The best advice I can give is just the op-

1961-1963 LINCOLN CONTINENTAL CONVERTIBLE: Perhaps the single most-collected car to date among motorcars of the sixties. By any standards, this car is a distinctive vehicle of great strength. Its open four-door configuration and fully concealable top quickly captured the hearts of fans of pre-WW II four-door phaetons. The sedan shares the same clean styling, frame strength and engine. The 1961-63 version is definitely preferable for appreciation potential; its shorter wheelbase (123 inches), curved side windows and unique dash design place it above the 1964-67 versions. The engine is a 430-cubic inch (seven-liter) V-8 of 300 hp at 4100 rpm. It has 465 ft-lb of torque at 2000 rpm! Weight: 5,115 pounds.

posite. Preserving some of these cars, which were the first to be factory-equipped with automatic transmission, power steering and brakes, four and six-way power seats, swivel seats, special radios, controlled interval wipers, air-conditioning, alternators, disc brakes, safety belts, etc., should be part of your accomplishment.

Select cars with all the accessories you can find, and then gradually pursue a plan of rebuilding the items until everything works like new again! To this end, you must have a positive, learning attitude about how your car's body is put together, and how its electrical components are wired. Life with your car can be enjoyable and economical once you know its few unique features and how to maintain them. An obscure hole near each wheel that catches street dirt and salt, or a power seat wire that *always* tends to fray can undermine your confidence in an otherwise reliable vehicle. It is not knowing, and not unscrewing a few bolts to find out, that causes unexpected disappointments. My personal approach, already discussed, is to buy only an original or properly-restored car, so you or your serviceman can focus attention on the small but essential details of thorough maintenance and upgrading — sort of a 'new used car' approach.

If your sole interests are driving and escaping that $1,200-plus annual depreciation of a new car, you certainly can have someone else attend to the actual maintenance. The key is having a bona fide program of care.

Even before you buy it's a good idea to

get out pencil and paper and evaluate all the parts of the car. Put it on a garage hoist, regardless of how little you know about what is under a car. Use your eyes. Ask questions if there is a mechanic around — two 'experts' are better than one. Take notes. Which parts are rusty? Which parts seem unusually oily? How's the muffler? Tail pipes? Tires? Then check the undercoating — way up into the wheel wells. Write more notes. As the car comes down from the hoist, check the chrome moldings and bumpers for rust. Stone chips? Are there any body panels along the bottom that pick up and hold water? And so on. Some engine diagnostic centers do no repair work. They are best for engine analysis, since they have no ulterior motive of generating business. They are hard to find, and I'm sorry I can't be more help there. You might try going into a diagnostic center and saying, "As a matter of principle, I want to have you examine my car, but I will have whatever repairs you advise done elsewhere. Will you do it?" For a flat fee they will; the cost will be worth it.

From day one, treat your new-found friend as a member of the family. Budget approximately ten percent of the car's original price per year to your maintenance and upgrading plan; it will do wonders. Go after the major items that affect safety or threaten other components immediately. A faulty hand brake ought to be fixed at once. Rank the list by the seriousness of the work. Many items, although you will eventually fix them, have no special priority in your budget. But don't end the year in black ink! Go back to your list and do a couple more items, unless you are holding some dollars back for a major project. I also spend a modest amount each year picking up parts before they are needed. On my Mercedes, I knew the electric fuel pump had been in the car since it was new (120,000 miles), and it was one of the few components essential to the engine's operation (warm engine starts) that had not been replaced. I bought one and kept it in the trunk until it was needed.

The ideal plan, then, might stretch out over the next several years, with a number of routine items fixed each year at standard mileage points. Big jobs and odd jobs will be scheduled at your convenience, unless they are safety items. This way you plan the car's fate, rather than the car planning yours!

Perhaps this plan sounds too complex. Not so. It is nothing more than an extension of the warranty maintenance plan the factory would expect you to follow to keep a new car standing tall.

The National Automobile Parts and Accessories Company (NAPA), while sometimes expensive, inventories parts for much longer than American car manufacturers and their dealers. Tune-up kits, gaskets, rubber fittings, chassis parts and bearings are available right off the shelf for cars built in the thirties, forties and fifties. The hobby magazines listed in Chapter 6 have ads by many firms specializing in specific years and models.

An example: In Minnesota's Twin Cities, Ford owners go to a place called Little

Dearborn. These friendly folks have made a business of buying up 'obsolete' Ford parts from dealers throughout Minnesota and other states. From a two-passenger Thunderbird's trim moldings to early Tin Lizzie parts, they usually can reach up on their shelves and bring down the part you seek. Sunday newspapers around the country frequently have ads by firms specializing in classic and postwar cars.

Another firm in Minneapolis, Metro Molded Parts, offers hundreds of replacement rubber fittings from foot pedal pads to door seals and gravel shields. Most cities have a few such specialized businesses, along with a few that will take on total restoration.

Original manuals, parts books and owners' manuals are advertised for the most obscure models. These are *must* items for both historical value and practical service advice. Twenty years from now, cars accompanied by all the manufacturer's manuals will have a distinct edge. Get the manuals now. Manufacturers' literature is a collector's field in its own right.

Those of you who have leather upholstery in your cars will want to obtain a catalog from The Clausen Company, 1055 King George Road, Fords, New Jersey 08863.

A useful step is to find a mechanic who serviced your model when it was new, or to locate a shop specializing in collectible cars. The Milestone Car Society has undertaken a nationwide listing of technical experts for most of the cars they have certified. Problems can be discussed by phone or letter. Overall, I can report a very positive spirit among collector car owners about both parts and service availability. Plugging into this subculture of other owners and establishing an intelligent preventative maintenance and improvement plan is the key to a permanent asset.

14 Chemical Dependency

Silicones, waxes, solvents, cleaners, preservatives, sealers, dyes, paints, naval jellies, rust inhibitors, greases, petroleum and synthetic lubricants are among (or should be) your car's 'habit.'

If you haven't already designated a large cupboard to inventory the many fluids and cosmetics your car loves, consider doing so soon.

Believe it or not, the more you are into automobiles, the more of a chemist you will become. Like most people, I started by reading labels on wax cans. To believe the labels, they're all best, slipperiest and fastest. Ditto for motor oils. If one seemed slightly more believable than another, or had a lower price, or a beautiful four-color photograph of a Mercedes-Benz SSK, it became my choice. Gradually, my experience with different products built my knowledge. Infrequently, someone writes a technical article in a car hobby magazine, which I plow through.

I parallel the progress and promotion of these chemicals for cars to the progress in automobile design. They change more often than they improve! If labels are glib, and meaningful changes scarce, where does this leave the car owners? With a dehydrating car? Well, that's what would happen if the owner does nothing. Just like human beings, if our cars are to survive they need protection from the weather outside, and from congestion and rot inside. The ideas that follow emphasize chemicals you should keep on hand and use.

Undercarriage — Rust Prevention

Beware of conventional undercoating. See the previous chapter for reasons and alternatives. Steam cleaning, sand blasting and naval jelly dissolve rust and all are useful. All will, however, damage wiring (especially the latter two). On a newly acquired collectible car, I would quickly attend to any rusty metal surfaces. After removing rust, coat with (1) *phosphoric acid* and (2) *zinc chromate primer* or rustproofing type primer. Be careful to use a primer that will be compatible with the final coat's ingredients. Independent consumer product testing during late 1975 ranked Sherwin-Williams Rust Control Primer No. 49 as most effective among dozens tested.[15]

If your car is driven in bad weather, consider spraying the entire undercarriage (except muffler) with LPS No. 3. This is a nondissolving, metal-preserving oil that does not slag (run) and remains effective for one to two years. Apply it every six months and rust won't have a chance.

Doors — Rust Protection, Rattles and Resonance

The inside bottom edges of doors rust if moisture collects. This occurs when leaves and rain fall into the window slots and the drain holes in the bottom of each door become blocked. On newly acquired, used vehicles, the inside door paneling should be removed and the insides repainted. Done properly on a four-door sedan, repainting may take more than ten hours; but the ultimate survival of your doors demands it. Rust from the inside out is very difficult to reweld if it deteriorates too far. After that first year's repainting, annually flood the bottom inside edge of each door with a quart of common motor oil if the car is driven regularly. Plug the drain holes with adhesive tape and saturate this critical spot. Drain after one-half hour and move to the next door.

Rockerpanels — Rust Prevention

In some cars, inspection holes into the rocker panels are located under the step-plates of each door. If there are no holes, take a saber saw and make them. The same routine for doors applies here. Manufacturers rarely paint these inner surfaces. You should. Oil annually if the car sees any weather.

Trim Moldings and Chrome — Rust Prevention and Shine

To prevent any rust at the clips or

nuts holding chrome moldings in place after rust removal and repainting, back all fasteners with zinc washers. *Zinc* is a sacrificial metal; it will rust instead of the car body.

Your chrome is most likely pot metal or stainless steel. The difference is vast. Stainless steel requires almost no care and it will buff out to a staggering shine. Pot metal is rarely adequately plated and pits easily, even in storage. One metal refinishing shop in five can re-chrome your pot metal, and the cost is usually as high or higher than seeking new-old-stock parts. Pot metal can be welded, though only a few dozen people in the world know how to do it correctly; their methods should be shared or franchised! A third type of bright-work is chrome-plated brass. It is the rarest, most expensive and most durable. The key to bright-work preservation is waxing, to keep it insulated from air and scratches.

Painted Surfaces — Preservation and Shine

Original paint should be preserved on cars as long as possible. Don't repaint a car at the first sign of cracking; a few hairline cracks in older paint adds maturity to a vehicle! Classic Car Wax Company has a paint restoring compound that is unusually good. If your car's surface is insulated from air and moisture by good waxing (many coats), the life span is indefinite. Don't push your luck by parking a valuable car in hot sunlight day after day, or by parking under trees that drip sap, requiring frequent rewashing or soaps. They remove the wax.

Glass Surfaces — Water Repellent and Anti-Fog

You may have seen ads for silicone-base glass polishes and paraffin-base substances to prevent window steaming. They both work. Silicone-base polishes will make your windows sparkle and repel staining water for months. It even works on the windows when the windshield wipers are used.

1940 LINCOLN CONTINENTAL: A perfect testimonial to this chapter, this beauty owned by Kermit Wilson, Minneapolis, is driven winter and summer! Your author discovered quite by coincidence that Mr. Wilson has practiced this chapter's rust prevention suggestions for years. Look at the results. These original Continentals were among the first eight automobiles exhibited by the Museum of Modern Art for their "excellence as works of art." Between 1940 and 1948, 5,324 were built, all with V-12 engines. The rarest year was 1942, when 336 were built. Also rare were 1940 models; 403 were built. Original price climbed to more than $4,500 by 1948. A staunch Lincoln Continental Owner's Club has only recently acknowledged the existence of other Lincolns. The 3,010 Mark II Continentals built in 1956-57 are also building a following. I suspect Mark III and Mark IV enthusiasts will also emerge, though seventies' Continentals have overplayed the Continental image to the point of humorous stereotype.

Paraffin is rubbed on the inside of the glass windows and prevents steaming from breath on cool mornings.

Leather and Vinyl — Preservation and Shine

Both leather and vinyl can last indefinitely. I have seen some beautiful interiors that are more than fifty years old. First, leather must be fed. Every three to six months all authentic leather must be coated with Lexol, Clausen's Rejuvenator Oil or a similar product. While this advice seems obvious, I see too much dry leather in fine cars *not* to emphasize it. I have mixed emotions about saddle soap; I don't have much success cleaning dirt out of the pores of leather with it. A stronger solution is sometimes required, but that is O.K. as long as it is rinsed off and followed by oiling. Vinyl does not breathe or absorb fluids as leather, but cracks do seem to be preventable when it receives the same treatment as leather. Ditto for stitching on seams. If leather is pleated, it is important to keep it clean all the way down into every seam or the stitching will rot. Leather coloring can be custom matched by the Clausen Company, Fords, New Jersey, by clipping a small sample of the color from under a seat and sending it to them. Their product is an elastic coating, not a dye. The firm also has a crack-filling compound for leather.

Fabrics — Preservation and Appearance

Original fabrics, especially those used after 1945, have unique patterns and are nearly impossible to authentically replace. If your fabrics are in good condition, modern car chemicals will help preserve them. After thorough cleaning of a solid color, consider spray dyes to correct fading. Also consider Scotchguard or clear plastic seat covers.

Engine Lubricants — Engine Life and Operating Efficiency

The use of petroleum lubricants in engines is rapidly outliving its suitability: Petroleum oil has poor tolerance for modern engine temperatures. Even when cars are stored, premium oil breaks down and loses viscosity. The American Petroleum Institute still recommends oil changes every three months despite manufacturer's extended-use claims. Post-1950 cars are prime candidates for *di-ester based synthetic motor oils*. In regular automobile use, 25,000 miles per oil change is possible. In collector-type cars, five-year intervals between oil changes are sometimes safe. Caution: If your engine already has (1) deteriorated engine parts or gaskets or (2) faulty carburetion which allows gas to dilute the oil, don't convert to synthetic oil. In short, don't neglect your engine oil — give some of the new lubricants close consideration.

Transmission and Power Steering — Life Span

Both these units' lubrication should be replaced every 25,000 miles. It rarely happens. When purchasing a used motorcar, change these oils as soon as possible on the assumption that the task has been neglected. Power steering units frequently have a filter that needs replacing, too. If either unit leaks, try the special conditioners available. They are beneficial if damage is not great. They help clean accumulated varnish from key parts and sometimes revitalize gaskets.

Differential — Preservation and Quietness

Watch for telltale leaks on the pavement around the differential, and check the fluid level whenever the chassis is lubricated. Replacement parts can be expensive and hard to obtain for some kinds of cars, though differentials are generally not troublesome. *Synthetic gear oil* is now available for differentials and conventional transmissions. It allows easier shifting and less roll resistance in cold weather, and life span is quadrupled.

15 Service and Restoration Shops Emerge

Throughout the nation, rather remarkable businesses are springing up that cater to the needs of owners (and buyers) of cars described in this book. Marion and Bud Josey are typical examples. They began as hobbyists in 1959 in Dunedin, Florida. Today their firm, Horseless Carriage Shop, is one of the finest and largest in the world. The color folder they have prepared to describe their services is impressive: To quote,

> Visitors are always welcome to tour the complex and view the 20 to 25 Antique, Classic and Special Interest Cars in various stages of restoration. When a car is brought in for restoration, it is completely disassembled and the various parts are then directed to their individual department where they are restored to like-new condition, yet keeping them as original as possible.
>
> Seats and interiors are sent to the upholstery department. The body

is lifted off the chassis, sent to the sandblasting shop, then to the wood-shop, if wood replacement is necessary. It then goes to the body shop for necessary repairs and on to the paint shop. After the chassis is dismantled completely, the related parts such as front and rear axles, springs, brackets, braces and the frame itself are all sent to the sandblasting shop where all rust and paint are removed to the bare metal before going to the body and paint shops. Engine, transmission and all other mechanical parts are sent to the automotive machine shop to be rebuilt. All engines are rebored, cams reground, crankshaft turned, new pistons, rings, valves and valve springs installed and when the engine is painted and reassembled, it is then placed on the engine dynamometer and broken in and tested before reinstalling it in the chassis.

After each department has completed the necessary work on the related parts, they are sent to the main assembly area to be re-assembled. When the restored car is finished and ready to leave the shop, it is in better than new condition. It is not uncommon to see cars sent in by owners from Foreign Countries for restoration, or to see Foreign buyers looking over the selection of Antiques and Classics for sale.

Another fine facility is Jack Wishuick's Roaring 20 Auto Museum, Wall, New Jersey, which houses more than one hundred great automobiles of the past, many of which are available for purchase. Places such as these are a great help in deciding which car(s) excites you most. The cross-section of cars to be seen usually ranges all the way back to the 'brass era,' when all fittings (lights, handles, etc.) were brass instead of chrome. I am not exaggerating when I say that high-caliber shops dealing (often exclusively) in collector cars have emerged in almost every major city and state in the nation: Jim Southard's Classic Car Investments of Atlanta; Ed Jurist's Vintage Cars of Nyack, New York; Robert Turnquist's Hibernia Auto

ROARING 20 AUTOS: In New Jersey, Roaring 20 now occupies the beautiful new building pictured here, containing both a museum ($2.50 admission) and a sales outlet. A large percentage of the vehicles are of vintages described in this book. Color catalogs of cars, with selling prices, are available for $10. Location of the Antique Auto Museum is on Route 34, one mile south of the Garden State Parkway, Exit 98, Wall, New Jersey 07719. Phone: (201) 681-8844.

Restorations, Hibernia, New Jersey; Automobile Classics in Santa Monica, California; Egge Machine Company, Gardena, California (an outstanding engine parts source); Arthur Rippey's Veteran Car Sales in Denver; and James Leake's Antiques Inc. of Muskogee, Oklahoma. All have good reputations.

Look for firms near you advertising in the magazines listed in Chapter 6, and in your local Sunday newspaper's classified ads under 'antiques' and 'classic cars.' (If your paper hasn't established such a classification yet, all I can say is that it's missing the boat.)

16 A Personal View on Automobile Design

What is a great automotive design anyway? To watch the ads, every vehicle is a brilliant break-through in function and beauty. The truth is that many pressures are at work to alter even the finest products. In hindsight many of the milestones of motordom barely made it to production and didn't last long. Even where enthusiasm is high, frequent model changes are programmed to phase out the good with the bad in the name of progress. All things otherwise being equal, the public tends to buy that which 'appears' new and fresh.

In Chapter 2 I described two styling strategies — programmed annual changes, and static design programs. In the latter, an 'ultimate' concept is sought; a design that does its job so well that it does not get old. This was the intent of the MK II Continental. Manufacturers have learned that the public consumes elegance and perfection almost as fast as mediocracy. It is a rare body styling feature that achieves much permanence. When the 1974

NASH-HEALEY: Another fine Pinin Farina body, this design won first place in Italy's International Concours d'Elegance on styling in 1953. In its class at Le Mans, Nash-Healeys placed fourth in 1950, sixth in 1951 and third in 1952, where, according to Donald Healey, the car used no water or oil during the entire twenty-four hours. The original 1951 cars had aluminum bodies. A total of 506 were sold by the end of the series in 1954. The car featured careful body detailing; lush, full leather; handmade hardware; and specially designed carpeting in the passenger compartment and trunk. The association with Pinin Farina was a significant chapter in Nash's history. The Nash-Healey's engine and suspension were extremely durable. One owner reported, "I personally used a 1953 hardtop at work for fourteen years, never garaging it. I put 147,000 miles on the engine before rebuilding." The engine was a 234.8-cid, overhead-valve, six-cylinder with 125 hp. A few 252.6 engines with 140 hp appeared in 1953-54. Top is a 1953 roadster. Bottom is a 1954 coupe.

Lincoln body stayed the same as the 1973, sales slipped, despite a superior product in all other respects. The body was redesigned in 1975 and sales doubled. Even though there is mutual public and professional agreement that certain designs transcend time, the public buys change. What's a mass production manufacturer to do?

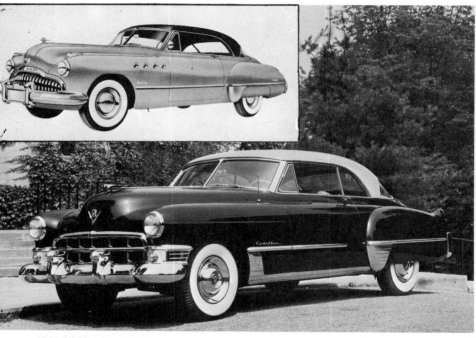

1949 CADILLAC COUPE DE VILLE: This was GM's first year to build a pillarless two-door hardtop; they made 2,151. The design was also available in the Buick Riviera and the Oldsmobile Holiday in the same year. The initial push for GM's adoption of the window treatment came from Harlow Curtis, just before he left Buick to become president of General Motors. Pontiac, Chevrolet and DeSoto added it to their lines in 1950, Ford and Plymouth in 1951. Chrysler did build seven bona fide hardtops in 1947, but GM must be credited with the first serious production. This Cadillac featured the first American overhead valve V-8; it produced 160 horsepower. Wheelbase: 126 inches. (The single 60S Coupe de Ville built had a wheelbase of 133 inches. Does anyone know where this car is today?) Photo inset: 1949 Buick's companion pillarless hardtop, the first Riviera. The two GM divisions shared some body parts, but engines and transmissions were totally different. All 1949 GM hardtops are *extremely* rare.

While auto builders continue on their merry chase, it remains for *us* to capture a few of the 'great ones.' And it is possible to make such distinctions. The Milestone Car Society certification criteria may be as good a measure as we'll find; it determines excellence in engineering, performance, innovation, craftsmanship or styling. The ultimate cars excel on all five points:

Some Five Point Milestones

1952–55 Bentley Continental series R
1951 Bugatti 101 and 101C
1953 Buick Skylark
1948–49 Cadillac
1946–49 Cisitalia GT coupe by Pinin Farina
1955–64 Citroen DS-19
1936–57 Continental Mark II
1951–55 Cunningham sports

1953 BUICK SKYLARK CONVERTIBLE: Top-of-the-line for Buick's Golden anniversary year, the Skylark also carried the first V-8 in Buick's history. It had a 188-hp, valve-in-head engine of 322 cubic inches, and the year's highest compression ratio, 8.5:1. Appointed as a Roadmaster, the 1953 Skylark was substantially more imposing than the 1954 version, which was built on the smaller Special chassis.

1961–64 Jaguar XK-E
1952–58 Mercedes-Benz 300S &
    300Sc
1954–63 Mercedes-Benz 300SL
1951–54 Nash-Healey
1951–58 Pegaso
1948–64 Porsche series 356
1953–54 Riley 2.5 Sports Sedan
1963–64 Studebaker Avanti

Sometimes one feature is so impressive that it is all that is needed. If the original M.G. TC was powered by a lawnmower engine, I think its styling would still command great respect. Come to think of it, I believe they *did* use lawnmower engines . . . I never heard of a TC engine lasting more than 30,000 miles without major work. Their suspension had the firmness of a buckboard, and availability of

1961-72 JAGUAR XK-E: A collector car of much repute due to its styling, engineering, performance, innovativeness and craftsmanship. This car's original 230-cubic inch engine delivered 265 hp and 150-mph speeds. Wheelbase: 96 inches. Maintenance on Jaguars is higher than on American makes, though Jaguars are still economical in the context of the $10,000-plus cars with which they are compared. Good parts sources are scarce, so well-preserved cars are substantially more valuable than worn examples. Available in both roadster and coupe (shown) versions.

M.G.: The car that started America's love affair with foreign automobiles. During the late forties and early fifties, M.G. outsold all other foreign cars in the U.S., and paved the way for Volkswagen's subsequent dominance. Frankly, these are rather primitive machines with hardly any trunk space, poor foul-weather protection, a very rough ride and uncertain engine life — yet the car's appearance melts everyone's reason in seconds. A wonderful toy! Very active owner's clubs exist with chapters throughout the world. Above: M.G.-TF. Below: M.G.-TC.

parts still breaks all records for slowness. No matter. You'll rarely find an M.G. owner who considers these drawbacks important. They are hopelessly in love with its striking appearance. I found myself on the verge of love with one this past summer . . . an M.G. TF. A red one. I didn't buy it. I looked at it too objectively and discovered the nearest thing it had to a trunk was only large enough to carry side curtains (you remember what side curtains are). The windshield wiper was hand-operated too! Of course, nowadays no one would take one of these M.G.'s out on a rainy day anyway. (Though I'm not sure whether that's to preserve the vehicle or because all the owners are still waiting for instructions on how to erect the top.)

This example of the M.G.'s strength and weaknesses pertains to most collectible cars. One or two aspects will excel, and attract recognition out of proportion considering the car's total merits.

Balance seldom occurs. Swedish auto builders have been hung up on engineering. The French give astonishing importance to innovation. Detroit's hang-up during the past twenty-five years has been body styling. It has taken public legislation to affirm such elementary engineering values as safety, fuel efficiency, and noise standards.

The tendency for cars of various nations to emphasize certain characteristics reflects the values of those respective countries. The nature of the people affects their finished products.

To make a quick tour of world automotive design, we will briefly review American, Japanese, English, Swedish, German, French and Italian designs.

AMERICA: Detroit has done very well designing their cars considering a rule they apply that started back in the thirties: "Make 'em different each year, different enough so that Jones can see that Smith has a new one — but not so different that I can't unload Jones' heap on Brown down the street!"[16] Economically, that has become a cornerstone in the U.S. policy of planned obsolescence, according to author Vance Packard and other authorities.

Another well-known phrase describing U.S. development is 'conspicuous consumption.'[17] Actually, for all the criticism Detroit (and all American industrial designers) receives, the idea has been a tremendous success. Manufacturers cannot defend themselves; to do so would be a confession of planned obsolescence. Yet conspicuous consumption and planned obsolescence stimulate our economy as much as profits. The faster money and products change hands, the more the country prospers. The affluence of our society stimulated this philosophy for many decades until the worldwide economic slow-down of 1973–75. This has seemed to make the U.S.A.'s frequent auto changes somewhat justified in that the by-product of jobs and easy access to products had greater value than the product itself.

The flaw which has undermined the cycle is abdication of other standards. Need for

1958 OLDSMOBILE 'CLUTTERBUILT': America's styling blunders certainly rival Sweden's Saab (below) for ironically opposite reasons. Theoretically, the highest emphasis in the USA has been placed on styling, while Sweden's focus has been on engineering. Walter Teague's fifth ingredient of good design, beauty, has often failed to materialize under either philosophy. The demoralizing fact is that sales are maintained less by beauty in design than they are by change itself — change of any kind permitting the product to be called 'new.' The 1958 Oldsmobiles broke sales records throughout the year. Air suspension (choke) was among the accessories offered.

SAAB 93: Built in Sweden, this ranks among the world's homeliest cars. Though these cars were mechanically innovative and durable, body designing was persistently misplaced in the hands of airplane engineers. Engines were equally unorthodox, including a two-cycle, two-cylinder model; a three-cylinder series; and a V-4. All had front-wheel drive and unit body construction. Torsion bar suspension was used on the models 92 and 93. Wheelbase: ninety-seven inches.

safety, fuel efficiency, rust prevention, to name three, were underestimated. Now, we've lived far enough into the seventies to realize the misjudgments. Add to this the air pollution problem, escalating production costs, and the end of the post-WW II baby boom (fewer and fewer teenagers to become drivers); overall, Detroit's long-range planners aren't too excited about continuing tradition. This cuts beyond the auto industry itself to a fundamental shallowness of the profit motive: Return on investment to stock holders has driven corporations to ever-increasing production, market share and profit margins at the expense of all other values. What Detroit needs now is a close look at companies like Maytag, which has learned how to live with more harmony of values among customers, employees and stockholders.

Despite America's attraction to new body styling , there are not many truly 'beautiful' Detroit automobiles introduced each year. According to Walter Teague, this is because their "designers are seldom, if ever, allowed to design or develop their own concepts of a car completely and present it as a finished working prototype to his bosses . . . take it or leave it as is, yet, this is the only way a designer should work." He goes on to support this statement by saying, "It is the way practically all successful designs are accomplished, by independent designers . . . by Henry Dreyfus, David Chapman, Peter Muller-Munk, and it is the way design is understood at General Electric, both at Bridgeport and at Louisville under Arthur Bec-

Var and Don McFarland; at Bell Telephone Laboratories under Henry Dreyfus; at IBM under Elliot Noyes; at Eastman Kodak under the general supervision I [Teague] have experienced there for 32 years."[18]

A few examples of typical American designs are pictured. Of course, there are exceptions.

With this background, let's move on to the foreign countries, where more cars are designed by individuals, instead of committees or styling sections.

JAPAN: Japan's post-WW II motorcar history is brief, though rapidly becoming significant. Styling in Japan has reflected American tastes and manufacturing processes more promptly than other nations. It is not yet possible to single out design traits unique to Japan.

1961 IMPERIAL CROWN CONVERTIBLE: Designed by Virgil Exner, this may have been Imperial's most opulent year. For Cadillac it was 1959, for Lincoln 1960. The myth that size equals excellence has been slowly dying. Nostalgia for the myth, however, will last forever. This model had a 350-hp V-8 from 413 cubic inches. Pistons were aluminum. Wheelbase: 129 inches.

By and large the Japanese get good marks in engineering, performance and innovation. They were leaders in marketing the Wankel and the stratified combustion engines. Economy has been a dominant theme, but that is not unique. Unquestionably, their most brilliant and successful auto design to emerge to date is the Datsun 240Z sports car.

ENGLAND: To quote Walter Teague again, there are five basic design objectives: efficiency, convenience, economy, simplicity and a fifth. The first four can be attained by an analytical approach; they require a high degree of intelligence and a sturdy conscience, but not genius or talent. If these were all the

JAGUAR XK 120 CABRIOLET: Offered from 1948 through 1954, during which years the XK 120 became the standard sports car for comparison. The few that upstaged it were substantially more expensive; one of Jaguar's fortes has been moderate price tags·for what it offers. Temperamental? By American standards, yes; though if you own a racehorse, treat it like a racehorse and you'll get along just fine. Initially a 210-cubic inch (3.4-liter) six-cylinder engine — generating first 160, then 180 and 210 horsepower — the Jaguar delivered more than 120 mph top speed. Weight: 3,100 lb; twenty-four gallon fuel tank; twelve-volt electric system. Wheelbase: 102 inches. Available as coupe, cabriolet and roadster. The first 200 roadsters were aluminum. These cars were extremely slow to drop in value — they are now rising much more quickly.

designer accomplished he would achieve a sound, pedestrian result, blameless but not admirable. But there is a fifth ingredient of really good design, which is unpredictable and delightful, and can't be worked out by any deductive or slide rule method. It is the personal flash of inspiration which the designer contributes out of his inner resources, which arouses the "keen sense of pleasure we call beauty."[19]

Unfortunately, many English designs of the pre-1970 period lacked this fifth ingredient, beauty. British auto history is full of homely cars.

The Allard was seen on racing circuits during the early fifties. This was followed by the Triumph TR series. Today the world's roads are full of odd English cars.

MORGAN: These cars are still being built with the same care and odd frames that distinguished the first products of Harry Morgan in 1911. Owners are as ardent as they come, keeping in close communication with the founder's son, Peter. Rather than retool for the USA's present new car import tests the factory frequently performs total restorations of older cars that are returned to Malvin Link in Worcestershire, England. The example shown is new, available with Rover V-8 power, producing 0-60 mph acceleration in 7.5 seconds. Wheelbase: ninety-eight inches.

Two examples of British 'butcherman-ship' are the Daimler SP 250 and the Austin 850. The Austin 850 has an efficient, economical and simple engine — mounted sideways, across the front axle, with front wheel drive.

Jaguar is one of the few exceptions in England . . . and it fits Walter Teague's design principle cited earlier: It's a one-man design by Sir William Lyons.

SWEDEN: I go next to Sweden because

VOLVO 1800ES SPORTWAGON: This well-received wagon barely got into production when additional U.S. safety standards caused Volvo to forego necessary retooling. Only 4,500 were built, mostly during 1972, making this the rarest of all Volvos. Full leather interiors, factory air conditioning, fuel injection and a choice of transmissions make for civilized, high-quality motoring . . . in a car that's likely to climb in value every year it is driven. Engine is a two-liter, four-cylinder. Wheelbase: 96.5 inches.

their designs are changing and improving, but still marginal. The well-known Volvo PV544 two-door sedan (commonly accused of being a shrunken 1941 Ford) is not a very graceful design, though it has remained in demand because it runs so well.

Saabs are built using aerodynamic theory (wind tunnel tested — similar to Porsche) by a sound company (a builder of jet airplanes), but they do not have that keen sense of pleasure we call beauty.

The latest Volvo and Saab models show some improvement, though they remain rather too businesslike to excite the bloodstream. Even the Volvo P-1800 ES sports car cannot be called beautiful.

The Swedes admire German workmanship. Both countries still have fine steel, and a few dedicated workers are still available (or their factories are more effective in motivating them, whichever is the case). Northern Europeans are domesticated to an extent by their socialized governments; domesticity is also reflected in their automobiles. The Swedes make no convertibles and only a few sun roof models. To this day, less than twenty-five percent of the cars on Swedish roads have automatic transmissions. Swedes wouldn't want to go out by a fjord with some new-fangled device.

Industrial conservatism also makes Sweden reluctant to try American-type yearly body changes; history is showing the prudence of this. Some English manufacturers try yearly model changes, though their volume per year hardly justifies the variations.

GERMANY: Moving southward, the Germans make few actual sports cars, and their sun roof and automatic transmission models sell better. The Germans are among the world's great machinists. They are fantastically thorough in all of their work. On race days back in the fifties, for example, the Mercedes-Benz factory teams even resorted to "motion pictures to analyze pit movements of their own and competitor's teams," and to give drivers film previews of the route to be covered in open-road racing events.[20] Today they take motion pictures to study such things as the action of suspension systems in cars on the road. Wind tunnel designing is a logical method for the Germans, and somehow they end up with more pleasant-looking wind tunnel designs than the Swedes.

GRAND MERCEDES PULLMAN: A rare press-release photo of the interior of this extremely luxurious automobile. Rear seats as well as front seats had power-operated angle adjustments. Other features included hydraulic door latches and air suspension.

GRAND MERCEDES: The front page of the model 600's catalog reads: "The history of the automobile is determined by the cars that make history." In the author's opinion, all the cars mentioned in this book will make history; though perhaps no firm has tried so hard (since 1945) to build a truly great car as has Mercedes-Benz. If they have a weakness, it is probably a lack of beauty in their designs — and this, in typical Mercedes-Benz self-awareness, is openly admitted in their ads: "Mercedes-Benz does not look like one of the greatest performing cars in the world. It merely is." Hydraulic power-assists, somewhat unsuccessful in their first appearance in cars before 1950, later took on prominence in commercial jet aircraft. This trend prompted Citroen and Mercedes to lead the way back to major automotive applications. In the 600, everything from door latches and front and rear seat-adjusters to the thermostatically-controlled engine fan was hydraulically powered. A 386-cubic inch (6.3-liter), overhead-cam V-8 engine delivered 300 hp at 4100 rpm. Torque was 434 ft-lb at 3000 rpm; maximum rpm was 4800. Top speed was 124 mph. Wheelbase on the sedan was 126 inches; on the limousine, 153 inches. Sedan weight was 5,380 pounds and the fuel capacity was 29.6 gallons. Introduced in 1964, the earlier models will represent exceptional investment opportunities for the next few years. However, anticipate eight to ten percent of original selling price for annual maintenance if you drive the car 10,000 miles per year; and avoid becoming involved in a restoration effort.

The original 300SL and the Porsche are both reasonably pleasant designs. They are conservative and functional — and very slow to change — but definitely acceptable. It seems that the further south you go in Europe, the more colorful and exciting the cars become. Volkswagen's Beetle, like the Swedish Saab, is functional but not beautiful. The main reason for the Beetle's success is its engineering — it sells despite its looks.

BMW 3.0 CSI: How many cars that can reach 60 mph from a standing start in 7.5 seconds and can go up to 135 mph, can also average 22+ mpg? And this charmer meets the 1975 U.S. emission standards, too! Large books have been written about V-12 and V-16 engines, but the heritage and future of six-cylinder engines may prove proudest. From Tucker and 300 SL Mercedes to Rolls-Royce Silver Wraith and Citroen SM: Straight sixes, V-6's, opposed flat sixes persist in durability, economy, smoothness, speed and quietness. BMW's top-of-the-line six provides 220 hp from 184.4 cubic inches. Wheelbase: 103.3 inches. These coupes have a unique balance not achieved by BMW sedans.

FRANCE: What we just said about Volkswagen might be applied in reverse to some French makes. I think that they look very fresh and progressive, but are a little more mechanically delicate than German and Swedish cars.

Bugatti is probably the most loved car in the world. The insatiable craving for a Bugatti has led many people to desperate acts. Though, fortunately, the case of Violette Noxier of Paris is unique. In 1934 Noxier

CITROEN SM: Introduced in 1971 and chosen as the 1972 Car of the Year by *Motor Trend* magazine, the SM was the primary product of a now-defunct alliance between Citroen and the famous Italian firm of Maserati. The SM had Citroen's proven hydropneumatic steering and suspension system; a four-cam, 165-cubic inch, 2.7-liter, V-6 engine (larger engines were subsequently offered) with 180 horsepower; and a five-speed transmission. A top speed of 135 mph has been reported. Nearly everything about this car was unique, from variable-ratio steering to central warning indicators on the dash that announced malfunctioning subsystems. The author feels that both the SM and the DS series 'want to be handled,' and consequently excel on curved, mountainous terrain rather than on straight expressways. Wheelbase: 116 inches.

killed her father for money — to buy a Bugatti for her boyfriend. Many French cars are radical. The Bugatti was beautiful, elegant and flashy, but the sound of a 35B being fired up was a mad cacophony. The sound is not easy to describe. There are three themes: (1) The excruciatingly sharp crack of the exhaust (a high level *ripping* sound); (2) the characteristic *growling, rattling,* bucket-of-bolts noise of the roller and ball-bearing engine (a Bugatti in good shape always sounds like it is about to fly to pieces!); (3) a siren-like rising and falling *scream* of the supercharger.[21] I mention this because French cars are, as a group, above average in sophistication; regrettably, this cannot

BMW 3.0 CSI INTERIOR: The BMW 3.0 CSI takes a back seat to no one. All four passengers are given a sense of security unrivaled by most homes. An armrest emerges if needed, and usual features such as air conditioning are present. Craftsmanship is nearly impossible to fault.

be said for the servicemen called upon to maintain them around the world.

In fairness to the French, I must say their cars are the most difficult about which to generalize. Dutch Darrin told me recently that he regards the French Hispano-Suiza to be a finer automobile than the Duesenberg. The French range, from simple cars to the most complex, is unequaled. Ditto on styling.

ITALY: Here is Italy . . . the last country on our tour. Italian cars are consistently colorful and exciting. The Italians do a better job of meeting Walter Teague's fifth cri-

CITROEN SM INTERIOR: French innovation at its finest takes decades for most manufacturers to surpass. Instrumentation includes a Master Alert panel informing the driver when any of twelve subsystems need attention, including wear of the front brake pads. The oval steering wheel has a single spoke.

PININFARINA LINE

NOT EVERY AUTOMOBILE
IS DESIGNED BY PININFARINA
BUT PININFARINA IS PRESENT IN ALL

PININFARINA Turin Italy

terion than any other country. Almost without exception, Italy's cars are beautiful. This is so well accepted that when any major company needs outside help in a body design, it goes to Italy. Even some American designs have been developed there. Pinin Farina designed the Nash Airflyte body; Chrysler's special bodies were always done by Ghia; the German Volkswagen Karmann Ghia is an Italian design.

The British Aston Martin DB series also has its design roots in Italy. Ferrari, one of the

The man himself, **PININ FARINA,** posing with a **FERRARI SUPERAMERICA 400** shortly before his death. Continuing to flourish in his absence, his firm has had a profound influence on automobiles, worldwide. Car after car in this book reflects the Pininfarina touch — every nation and every decade places them in the forefront of the beautiful and exciting 'solutions.' The 1958 advertisement reprinted on the facing page remains quite true.

greatest cars in the world, has always carried clean, exciting, graceful shapes. The newest Pininfarina/Ferrari styling is on the leading edge of brilliance. Ford's de Tomaso Pantera is in the same school. Sure enough, Italian design.

I have not gone into mechanical features much, but a study would show that one

GHIA CROWN IMPERIAL LIMOUSINE: One hundred thirty-two Ghia-built limousines were manufactured by Chrysler between 1957 (pictured) and 1965. After that date they were built in America by Stageway Coaches, Inc. Many of the Ghia cars were hand modified, convertible frames with coupe bodies, stretched to limousine proportions. With Cadillac cornering ninety percent of the limousine market, Chrysler had to do something special to get attention — and special they were! What finer way to travel! Dual air conditioners were standard. Wheelbase: 149.5 inches. Virgil Exner directed styling. (He also did the Stutz Blackhawk shown elsewhere in this book.) Italian assembly was a blessing for all; the considerable labor involved in each car was accomplished by a skilled firm at a small fraction of what comparable work would have cost in America. Italian inflation has now erased that situation.

1957 DUAL GHIA: Built by Carrozzeria-Ghia of Torino, Italy. "Sports car styling with four-passenger comfort and utility," read their catalog. Available in both coupe and convertible, they were powered by 260-horsepower Chrysler V-8 engines through Powerflite automatic transmissions. These power plants were consistently chosen by special coachbuilders — in the Briggs Cunningham cars, the Jensen Interceptor II and III and Facel Vega's V-8's. The above model retailed for $7,889 f.o.b. Detroit (the American marketing point). Wheelbase: 115 inches; twelve-volt electrical system.

1953 CHRYSLER D'ELEGANCE. A rich man's Karmann Ghia, this car was one of an impressive series of design experiments conducted by Chrysler during the fifties. Most were one-of-a-kind creations that were sold in South America or Europe when Chrysler was done with them. The series inspired a small, hand-built production of 143 Dual Ghia motorcars and 400 GS-1 motorcars, the latter sold through Chrysler's French distributor, Societe France Motors. Almost all these cars used standard Chrysler V-8 motors with automatic transmissions. Wheelbases ranged from 105 to 129 inches. All are important collector vehicles.

man engineering designs are usually more temperamental, radical and harder to service. These radical designs are very efficient in accomplishing the *specific* task for which they were designed, but are marginal because of inconvenient serviceability. Engineering groups or committees are generally more apt to consider the disadvantages of exciting and radical approaches.

Considering the foregoing, what is the ultimate combination . . . committee-designed mechanical components beneath a stunning, private-studio-designed body? Support for this thinking is found in the French Facel Vega, which did all right as long as Chrysler Corporation engines and drive parts were used. The Facellia, a double overhead valve engine of Facel's own design, sunk the ship. Today the beautiful Avanti II (designed by Robert Andrews for Raymond Loewy's Studio) is being hand-built in Indiana with General Motors mechanical components and as far as I know is prospering, with many happy customers. The Jensen Interceptor II and III, and the Stutz Blackhawk are two beautiful offspring from the mating of committee-designed engines with custom bodies. They use Chrysler and GM mechanical components, respectively. The de Tomaso Pantera (Ford V-8 power) and the stylish Bricklin (AMC power) are two more examples. These motorcars are not built as disposable cars. They are equipped with the latest safety and anti-pollution devices, and are worth preserving and enjoying for a lifetime. If these

STUTZ BLACKHAWK: Originally conceived by Virgil Exner for a potential rebirth of the Duesenberg, the Stutz nameplate has again emerged. Hand-built in Italy with a General Motors chassis and engine, and nearly any interior variation one could desire. At a price of approximately $35,000, the car incorporates eighteen-gauge steel as well as mink carpeting. An excellent mix of custom design with proven, easy-to-service mechanical components. An appealing car, intentionally overpriced to insure exclusivity of ownership.

FORD'S 1973 DE TOMASO PANTERA, MODEL L: A short-lived dream that proved chances of new car survival are as poor with large companies as with small ones. Just more than 4,000 Panteras were built. This seems to be the upper limit of production for many special cars. . . . That there are limited numbers clearly increases the speed of appreciation (in hearts and pocketbooks). The car had a practical American Ford V-8 engine encased by one of Italy's finest automotive designers, Alejendro de Tomaso. It had a mid-ship engine, five-speed transaxle, air conditioning and even power windows. The ultimate Ford?

models are too expensive for your pocketbook, two suggestions: (1) re-read this book, wait in the bushes for any one of these beauties to take its usual irrational plunge down to your price level, and rescue it; (2) look around for lower priced examples of the same concept; e.g., the Volkswagen Karmann Ghia.

1956-1974 VOLKSWAGEN KARMANN GHIA: One of the most brilliant achievements of motordom. An ageless design largely hand-built, with chassis and engine by a major international manufacturer, all miraculously priced under $3,000. It was impossible to form some parts of the body on a press; these were welded together by hand, and sculptured to their final shape with hand tools and melted pewter, as in the world's most expensive cars. Detailing is impressive throughout. From the driver's seat not one Phillips head screw is visible. Horsepower increased over fifty percent during the two decades of production in two models, a coupe and a cabriolet convertible. Wheelbase: 94.5 inches.

Footnotes

[1] Peter Drucker, "Six Durable Economic Myths," *Wall Street Journal* (vol 55), September 16, 1975.

[2] "A Second Car That Pays for Itself," *Better Homes and Gardens* (vol 51), February, 1973, p 22.

[3] Judson Gooding, "The Moving Sculpture of Old Cars," *Fortune* (vol 88), September, 1973.

[4] L. L. Liston and R. W. Sherrer, *Cost of Operating an Automobile*, U.S. Department of Transportation (Washington, D.C.: U.S. Government Printing Office No. 875–490, 1974).

[5] Special study by Office of Consumer Services, State of Minnesota, 1972.

[6] 1949 Buick Riviera, 1949 Cadillac 60S, 1956 Continental Mark II, 1954 Jaguar XK 120M, 1954 Kaiser Darrin, 1956 Pontiac Safari, 1951 Jeepster, 1957 Eldorado Brougham, 1957 Chevrolet Corvette, 1953 Hudson Hornet, 1953 Kaiser Dragon, 1956 Mercedes Benz 300Sc, 1953 Studebaker Starliner.

[7] John Olson, "In This Corner," *Old Cars* (vol 4), February 25, 1975, p 25.

[8] William B. Mead, "Home Improvements for Love or Money," *Money* (vol 2), January, 1973.

[9] G. Marshall Naul, "How Rare It Is," *Special Interest Autos* (vol 3), April-May, 1972.

[10] "Mr. Auburn," *Old Cars* (vol 1), May, 1972, p 30.

[11] In a letter to the author.

[12] A non-profit organization called National Institute for Automotive Service Excellence, 1826 K Street N.W., Washington, D.C. 20006, has begun testing superior mechanics through written exams; however, this positive step doesn't solve the problems of flat rates (piecework) and commissions paid on parts used.

[13] Margaret Bresnahan with Ronald G. Shafer, *How to Get Your Car Repaired Without Getting Gypped* (New York: Harper & Row, 1973), $6.95.

[14] The 1953 Studebaker Starliner, credited throughout this book to Raymond Loewy, is technically the work of Bob Bourke and Holden Koto of Loewy's staff. While this circumstance is true for a number of famous designs, for simplicity the author has followed the practice of crediting only the studio principal.

[15] "Metal Primer Paints," *Consumer Reports* (vol 40), August, 1975.

[16] "The Responsibilities of the Industrial Designer," *Road & Track* (vol 5), January, 1960, p 46.

[17] Thorstein Veblen, *The Theory of the Leisure Class* (New York: Houghton-Mifflin, 1973).

[18] Walter D. Teague, in an address to the Detroit chapter, Industrial Designers' Institute, August 16, 1959.

[19] Ibid.

[20] Ronald Hansen, *Different Backgrounds Breed Different Philosophies on Racing* (New York: Scarlet and White, 1958), p 64.

[21] Ken W. Purdy, "The Fabulous Bugatti," *Kings of the Road* (New York: Bonanza Books, 1952), p 17.

Picture Acknowledgements

Allstate Insurance Company, Training Division: 53 top, 69 bottom
American Motors Corporation: 56, 64 top, 144 bottom
Bricklin Vehicle Corporation: 54 top
British Leyland Motors, Inc.: 148
Buick Division, General Motors: 32, 33
Cadillac Division, General Motors: 21
Chevrolet Division, General Motors: iv, 23 bottom
Chrysler Corporation Historical Collection: 5 top, 26, 43, 47, 153,
    167 top
Citroen SA of North America: 161, 163
John Conde, American Motors: 77
Daimler-Benz of North America: 46, 58, 158
Ford Motor Company: 22, 24, 25, 96, 124, 125, 169 bottom
General Motors, Photographic Section: 20, 39, 44 top, 59 bottom, 146
Theodore Hall: 8, 16, 23 top, 51 top, 53 bottom, 54 bottom, 65, 69 top,
    70 top, 72 bottom, 93, 144 top, 147, 167 bottom, 169 top
Mark Hebert: 63
Tim Howley: 49 top
The Idea Farm, NYC: iv top
Jensen Motors: 62
Kruse Auction Classics: 104
Edward Lane: 11
Richard Langworth: 5 bottom, 12, 13 37, 48, 141, 145, 154, 165, 166
Morgan Motor Company, Ltd.: 155

Oldsmobile Division, General Motors: 19, 27, 49 bottom, 151 top
Porsche-Audi Division, Volkswagen of America: 66 bottom
Richard Quinn, 19647 S. Wolf Road, Mokena, Illinois 60448: 45
SAAB-Scania Aktiebolag Ltd.: 151 bottom
Jim Sechser: 66 top
Volkswagen of America: 170
Volvo of America Corporation: 156
Kermit Wilson: 135

Index

SIGN OF THE TIMES: This advertisement appeared in the *Wall Street Journal* just before the first edition of this book went to press.

Text for this book was set in fourteen-point Baskerville. Captions were set in eight-point Univers. Printed and bound by North Central Publishing Company, St. Paul, Minnesota.